CRAWL
with
GOD,
DANCE
in the
SPIRIT!

A Creative Formulation of Korean Theology of the Spirit

JONG CHUN PARK

ABINGDON PRESS
Nashville

CRAWL WITH GOD, DANCE IN THE SPIRIT!
A CREATIVE FORMULATION OF KOREAN THEOLOGY OF THE SPIRIT

This book is printed on recycled, acid-free paper.

Library of Congress Cataloging-in-Publication Data

Park, Jong Chun. 1954—
  Crawl with God, Dance in the Spirit!
  ISBN: 0-687-056896

98 99 00 01 02 03 04 05 06 07—10 9 8 7 6 5 4 3 2 1

MANUFACTURED IN THE UNITED STATES OF AMERICA

Contents

CHAPTER 1

The Birth of the Third Theology

Introduction

THE THIRD THEOLOGY is the theology of the twenty-first century which is going to become the age of information. Theocentric theology appeared with the first wave of agricultural civilization and homocentric theology emerged with the second wave of industrial civilization. The third theology is a theology of the Spirit which goes beyond competitive relationships between God and humans in order to encourage cosmic and historical divine-human participation.[1]

A few theologians who are concerned about postmodernity have already suggested a new paradigm of theology which can solve the problem of holding divine sovereignty without loosing human freedom.[2] The orthodox line of Western Christian theology from Augustine to Barth has argued for divine sovereignty over against human freedom as we can observe in the conflicts of Augustinianism with Pelegianism, Calvinism with Arminianism, Barthianism with liberalism, etc. Historically, theological debates typical of the Western church have faced the dilemma of keeping divine sovereignty or losing human freedom and any theological imagining about divine-human participation or synergy has been condemned.

Augustine's doctrine of creation and Anselm's doctrine of atonement are good examples of the first theology. It emphasizes "creation out of nothing (*creatio ex nihilo*)" so that God's relationship with the world is unilateral. God is the absolute, unchangeable, impassible, and eternal being. The world is relative and changeable, and the human being is passable and finite. If God is omnipotent, why do we have evil in the world and sin among people? This theodicy question caused the modern form of atheism. The first theology never gave up its argument for the absoluteness of God because it was afraid that denying one-sided dependence of the world upon God would encroach on the realm of divine sovereignty. In the discussion of "Why did God become a human being? (*Cur deus homo?*)" it was maintained that God himself neither became finite nor felt any pain in the

7

process of incarnation and crucifixion, although it looked as if God suffered. This kind of argument cannot escape the old metaphysical framework according to which divinity is an independent unchangeable substance. Its forensic theory of atonement falls into objectivism without any human participation. The God of the first theology does not resemble the God of the Bible and is not relevant to the modern person's structure of understanding.

The emergence of the second theology was intertwined with that of the modern world. It was theology from below which was based on a philosophy of subjectivity and started with the religious experience of the human being. The historical fabric of the second theology was embroidered with Luther's theology of *sola fide,* the pietism of inward spirituality, and neo-Protestant liberal theology from Schleiermacher to Troeltsch. Luther's theology did not get rid of the vestiges of the first theology. His word view was pre-Galilean, and his political view was feudalistic and authoritarian. What made Luther's theology the starting point of the second theology was his discovery of existence before God (*coram Deo*). The second theology actually began after the Enlightenment, after the formation of modern rationalism. Both the modern person's belief in mechanistic law which rules material beings and the modern person's search for freedom and autonomy in the realm of the subjective spirit were at the bottom of modern civilization. Thus the dimension of religion was reduced to the inner world of subjectivity while the material world became the mere object of natural science. After Kant's critical philosophy overthrew the speculative system of old metaphysics, modern philosophy was divided into Kierkegaard's existentialism and Marx's historical materialism. The existence of God, which was considered the postulate of practical reason in the beginning of modern theology, was exposed as the mere safeguard of bourgeois morality in Nietzsche's nihilism.

Ecumenical Context

The birth of the third theology requires a new world view, a new humanism, and a new paradigm of theology. This great change is often compared with the coming of the third church and with the flooding of the third wave.[3] The third theology is not merely theology of the Third World. The third theology transcends geographical boundaries. It does not exclude First World theology which contributes to overcoming the defects of the second theology. The world has become one global village and geographical distance has been reduced by mass media and rapid travel. The encounter between the stories of God in the history of Israel and the lofty ideas of Greek and Roman thought produced the first theology. The key for creative formation of the third theology is the encounter between the stories of the experience of God in the history of Israel and the spiritual resources of Third World people which have been the wellspring of their liberation from the five-hundred-year history of suffering under the domination of Western and Japanese imperialism.

The paradigm shift from the second theology to the third theology presupposes the total crisis of life caused by the materialism of modern science, the homocentrism of modern theology, and the limitless growth of capitalist market economies. This crisis is most visible in the third world which has been exploited by Western colonialism. The JPIC (Justice, Peace, and the Integrity of Creation) movement launched by the WCC in the 1980s has succinctly demonstrated the tasks of contemporary theology and mission. The document of the 1990 JPIC world convocation held in Seoul begins with the phrase "Between the Flood and the Rainbow," which symbolizes that we are living with the total threat of life on the one hand and the divine promise of a new heaven and new earth on the other. The theological leitmotif of the document is "covenanting."[4] The act of making covenant which is demanded in the total crisis of life is to renew the original biblical covenant in order to enhance justice, peace, and the integrity of creation. This is a triple covenant between God and human beings, between human beings and other human beings, and between human beings and other creatures.

Just before the JPIC convocation, the "Baar Statement" was adopted in a conference held by the WCC.[5] Its central theme of interreligious dialogue is also illuminated by the ecumenical theology of covenant. The Noachian covenant is the cosmic covenant of God with all creatures. The theological ground of interreligious dialogue is not only the cosmic covenant made by God with Noah but also our faith in God the Creator who has been present and active in all creatures from the beginning of creation. It means that God's particular covenant with Israel and Jesus Christ does not contradict God's universal covenant with all creatures through the Holy Spirit.

The theme of the 1991 general assembly of the WCC was "Come Holy Spirit, Renew the Whole Creation!" It indicates a significant change of emphasis in ecumenical theology. The major theological subject matter implied in the themes of the WCC general assemblies had been Christocentric. Since the JPIC movement was launched after the 1983 general assembly, the theme of the Holy Spirit in relation to the JPIC process was adopted for the first time in the history of the WCC. The eighth assembly of the WCC which will be held in 1998 will celebrate the Jubilee of the WCC which was organized in 1948. The theme of the first assembly of the WCC was "Man's Disorder and God's Design," which reflects the

9

chaos of post World War II. Barth criticized the theme because it turned over the divine initiative.

Since the end of World War II, newly independent nations in the Third World had been divided by the two superpowers into opposing camps. Even after the downfall of the Eastern bloc and the Soviet Union, Korea is the only nation still divided by Cold War ideology. The NCCK announced the 1995 Jubilee year in its 1988 declaration of peace and reunification of Korea. The Jubilee metaphor has become the focus of ecumenical theology born in the Korean Christian praxis for the JPIC. The theme of the eighth general assembly of the WCC is "Turn to God, Rejoice in Hope." In 1994 the Central Committee of the WCC decided the theme of the next general assembly in full agreement with the spirit of the Jubilee movement in the Korean church. The general secretary of the WCC, Konrad Raiser, called for "the ecumenical Jubilee" in his keynote speech at the 1995 Jubilee conference in Seoul.[6] The ecumenical Jubilee is the most fitting metaphor for the next general assembly of the WCC which is the last general assembly in the 20th century and will mark a great turning point for the church in the third millennium.

Turn to God and Crawl With God!

When we discuss a possible globalization of local theology in Korea, there is no better theme than that of Jubilee which has grown out of Korean Christian praxis and can be ecumenically universal without minimizing the individuality of Korean Christian experience. Korean theology of the Spirit as the third theology has the task of understanding and interpreting the theme of the next general assembly in the light of Korean Christians' language and experience in order to contribute to the ecumenical Jubilee movement. The task is the deepening of the ecumenical Jubilee theme in connection with the root metaphors of Korean *minjung* Christians: crawl with God and dance in the Spirit!

"Turn to God" is the call for our repentance with the full assurance that God gives us the Jubilee of reconciliation and liberation in Jesus Christ. The call to the Jubilee which is linked with the day of atonement is an invitation to repentance. It has been proposed that the forthcoming assembly of the WCC be structured around a ritual of confession, forgiveness, and reconciliation in order to open the way for an act of unity at the end of a millennium of division and Christian expansion.

We could not turn to God unless God first turned to us in Jesus Christ. To talk of the turning or repentance of God seems absurd and even blasphemous. The Jubilee call is the call for a conscious self-limitation of power in terms of property titles and of domination over slaves in order

10

to restore a sustainable order of human community. But how could God call us to the self-limitation of power if God himself does not go through the same process of the self-limitation of power in Jesus Christ? There are a few postmodern theologians in the West who maintain the "surrelativity" of God in the sense that God's perfection lies in relativity as well as absoluteness. God is then "the self-surpassing Surpasser of all."[7] But it is not necessary for them to relate the surrelativity of God with the self-limitation of God in Jesus Christ. It is here that the third theology parts company with First World postmodern theology. There is no universal metaphysical principle of surrelativity which can be applied to the Christian conception of God. We rather start with the concrete historical experiences of God and seek their universal meaning in dialogue with the various thought paradigms available.

The model of the God of Jubilee cannot be discovered in the historical experiences of First World people who have conquered the non-Western world for the last five hundred years. Doing the third theology is not a matter of intellectually attractive thinking in one's armchair. It is committing oneself to a surprising discovery of the model of God in the language and experience of Third World people. They have crawled in their history of suffering and liberation. "There is a flying one over a crawling one" as a Korean proverb goes. The metaphor of a flying one refers to those who experience history as if it were a linear process of development. The metaphor of a crawling one refers to those who wander the margins of history as the Hebrews wandered the desert after their initial triumph of Exodus. The task of the third theology is to discover the traces of God's crawl which have been buried in the historical experience of those who have crawled over the hill of Arirang. The hill of Arirang is a legendary hill of resistance and suffering at the top of which innumerable righteous Koreans were executed by the corrupt officials of old Korea.

God of Jubilee takes sides with those who crawl in history and judges those who step on the crawlers and fly over them. At this juncture, it is misleading to relativize the evil in the name of universal love which is clearly shown in the *kenosis* (self-emptying) of God. The metaphor of the emptying God in Phil. 2 should not be misunderstood as the antinomian standpoint of universal compassion which tends to nullify justice issues by reducing the unredeemed anguish of victims into the abstract notion of universal or collective *karma*.[8] The crawling God should not be confused with the emptying God. By not taking sides with victims, the standpoint of universal love or compassion can be easily coopted by the standpoint of assailants. The metaphor of the crawling God is fitting to the understanding of the Philippian text in the sense that God humbled himself in

11

the incarnation and took sides with the humbled by taking the form of a slave. The word crawl means a movement or an action in an abjectly servile manner. The *kerygma* of God's becoming a slave must have been shocking and revolutionary in the age of slavery. God who crawled in Jesus Christ provides the *minjung* with courage to resist the tendency of resignation and fatalism or the cynicism of power.

Israelites indeed crawled over many hills of resistance and suffering in their history which had been constantly controlled or invaded by the imperial powers of the ancient Near East. During the Babylonian captivity, which lasted almost 50 years, a creative minority among Israelites pronounced the drawing of the messianic kingdom in the midst of their crawl. The messianic expectations were thoroughly imbued with the spirit of Jubilee. According to Luke 4, Jesus' messianic mission also implies the Jubilee tradition. A few verses in Psalms (22:6, 103:14, 119:25, 143:7, etc.) were the outcry of the crawling persons who were laid low in the dust. Those verses are postexilic. Especially the famous cry in Psalm 22:6 ("But I am a worm and not a man") presupposes the image of God's suffering servant in second Isaiah. His unjustifiable suffering was no longer considered God's punishment of his sins, but it was considered the expiatory suffering for the people of God. The image of the suffering servant of God refers to the presence of God who crawled with Israelites over the hill of resistance and suffering. Through the presence of God in the Israelites' crawl, the messianic hope was born. The Jubilee text in Leviticus 25 is a part of the Aaronic priests' documents to envision a new messianic community in the reconstruction of postexilic Israel. They discovered the prototype of messianic community in the wandering life of their ancestors which was centered at the tent of meeting. It is significant to note that it was not the Jerusalem temple but the wandering community around the tent of meeting in the Sinai desert that was the prototype of the messianic community. Jesus' messianic mission also struggled against the corruption of temple worship. Protestant reformers also fought against the Babylonian captivity of the true church. The third theology must resist the corruption of the third church which has become serious in the present Korean church.

In order to interpret 'turn to God" in terms of 'crawl with God" we have to go back to the early Korean Christians' original experience of the Gospel. The early Korean Christians, most of whom were the *minjung*, did crawl in their history of resistance and suffering. They were treated by Japanese imperialists as if they were worms, not men. It was Jesus Christ whose 'worm experience' in his crawl toward the cross touched the innermost spirits of the Korean *minjung*. The phenomenal achievement of a mass conversion of the Korean *minjung* since the Great Revival of 1907 was the consoling as well as convicting works of the Holy Spirit. Their turn to God, i.e., their repentance, was their crawl with God, i.e., their identification with the crucified Lord Jesus Christ. Great Korean revivalist Sungbong Lee (1900-1965) described the spirit of Korean Christians' suffering with Christ in his poem "A Lily among Thorns":

> A lily among thorns, a saint of the Lord
> 'Cause of the constant pricking pain,
> How many times you wept, nobody knows.
> The Lord will wipe out your tears.
>
> Let the southeast wind blow!
> Let the northwest wind blow!
> A lily among thorns, a bride of the Lord
> Spreads the charming fragrance all over.

"Like a lily among thorns is my darling among the maidens" (Song of Songs 2:2). This verse was frequently interpreted as Christ's confession of love to his beloved saints in the history of Christian mysticism. Sungbong Lee went a step further to delve into the depth of the suffering love of the saints who were fully united with Christ wearing the crown of thorns on his head. He felt that the southeast wind of Japanese and American colonialism as well as the northwest wind of Chinese and Russian imperialism blew on the tiny Korean peninsula. Korean Christians seemed to him like a lily among thorns or a bride of the Lord. So he could proclaim with courage: let the wind blow on the thorny peninsula and let the lily prove herself to be the bride of the thorn-crowned Lord!

The call for Jubilee is the call for repentance, for turning to God and crawling with God. And the call must "begin with the family of God" (1 Peter 4:17a). It must begin with the Korean church, only then can the call for the ecumenical Jubilee spread all over the third church. The Korean church must repent of forgetting the first love of the Lord. The evangelization of North Korea, Asia, and the rest of the third world should begin with Korean Christians turning to God in solidarity with the crawling people, such as the foreign migrant workers in South Korea, the starving North Koreans, and the poor in Asia.

Rejoice in Hope and Dance in the Spirit!

The year of Jubilee is the year of rejoicing in the hope that God the Creator restores wholeness of life. The Jubilee focus on redistribution of

13

the land aims at the sustenance of life. The affirmation that the land belongs to God means not only the restoration of the integrity of creation, respecting the sanctity of life as a gift from God, but also the implementation of justice and peace among nations. More than 500 years ago Western imperialists began to invade the Third World by usurping the land. The Christian mission, which went hand in hand with the colonialization of the Third World, could not help but remain incomplete because it aimed at the salvation of the souls of native people who lost their land. This Gnostic colonialistic mission, which was nothing but the betrayal of the Gospel, was challenged by the powerful resurgence of native religions such as Islam, Hinduism, Buddhism, and Confucianism. These native religions provided the spiritual resources for the national liberation movements representing the spirit of Jubilee in disguise. The historical failure of the Western Christian mission in Asia was caused by confusing commitment to the Gospel with the modernization of Asia on the one hand and by the lack of spiritual discernment of the multireligious situation on the other.

The Christian mission for the ecumenical Jubilee in the twenty-first century must combine commitment to the Gospel with spiritual discernment of the multireligious culture. In contemporary Asia, the Gnostic Christian mission, which imposes the Western form of Christianity on Asian culture, and the anti-Christian counter mission of resurging native religions are in tension and conflict. Within the Christian camp in Asia there are two contradicting theologies of mission. One is the pseudo-evangelical theology of mission which takes an exclusive attitude at worst and an inclusive attitude at best toward other living faiths in Asia. The other is the pseudoecumenical theology of mission which supports religious dialogue and religious pluralism at the cost of commitment to the Gospel.

Eastern Orthodox theologian Nicephorus talked of "the melody of theology" in the midst of his struggle against the iconoclasts. According to him, the icons are "expressive of the silence of God. . . .Without ceasing and without silence, they praise the goodness of God, in that venerable and thrice-illumined melody of theology."[9] If the melody of theology was crucial for the iconophile theology of worship, the rhythm of theology is essential for the third theology of mission. Think of the four beat rhythm of "Onward, Christian Soldiers" or "Stand up, Stand up for Jesus" which have been sung most frequently for the cause of mission. If non-Christian Asians despise these hymns, can you blame them for their ungrounded xenophobia? Do you have to march against them as if they were your enemies and even the enemies of God? Why do you not take another

14

approach to Asians who love to sing and dance? You cannot dance to the tune of a militant march. What you need is a venerable three-beat rhythm of theology.

How and where can we discover the venerable three-beat rhythm of theology through which we might overcome the conflict of two extreme beats of the Gnostic Christian mission vs. the anti-Christian counter mission of Asian religions and secular ideologies, or the conflict of the evangelical theology of mission vs. the ecumenical theology of mission? It is not a matter of reducing the neo-Manichian dualism of a two-beat theology into the monism of nature religions. It is rather a search for the third yet-fuzzy beat of the Spirit which helps us go beyond the arbitrary theology of divine sovereignty that victimizes human autonomy on the one hand, and the unruly theology of unitive mysticism that reduces divine initiative into religious intuition on the other. Only our honest and sincere striving to hold together in creative tension a true evangelical, personal spirituality and a true ecumenical, public praxis can make us sing and dance to the tune of a venerable three-beat theology.

Black theologian James Cone once mentioned that the history of African Americans is a black spiritual. The history of the Korean minjung is also a *minyo* (*minjung* song). The most popular and typical *minyo* is Arirang:

> Arirang, Arirang, Araryo
> Going over the hill of Arirang
>
> My lover leaving and going away
> Will have a swollen foot within ten li.[10]

The melody of Arirang is sad and melancholy because it conveys *han*, "a dominant feeling of defeat, resignation, and nothingness on the one hand, and on the other hand, a feeling of tenacity to struggle for life."[11] None of the Korean *minjung* sings Arirang without bodily motion. When they sing it, they cannot help feeling a mysterious pulse from the shoulder and eventually bursting into dance. It is caused by the unique three-beat rhythm called *semachi*. It is rather caused by a fuzzy but venerable beat of the Spirit which intercedes with groans for the downtrodden people crawling like worms in history. Yes, it is rather the amazing grace of God that "turns wailing into dancing" (Psalms 30:11).

But how can we expect that Vietnamese refugees will rejoice and dance? How can we expect that starving North Koreans will rejoice and dance? How can we expect that foreign migrant workers in South Korea, Japan, Hong Kong, and Singapore will rejoice and dance?

15

The joy of Jubilee was never actualized in history because the rich and the powerful never gave up their vested interests. A TV drama running this year in Korea is "Kwangcho Cho." This drama is about the sixteenth century social reform by neo-Confucian scholar Kwangcho Cho. Kwangcho Cho challenged the injustice caused by the aristocracy and based on the hereditary ownership of land and slaves. He dreamt of the world where the *chonmin* (the lowly people) could dance. When he was killed by his enemies in 1519, he was only thirty-eight years old. His death as well as many other righteous leaders' deaths during the old Korean dynasty meant the death of hope for the poor and lowly people. That is why the Korean *minjung* sang their Arirang: "My lover leaving and going away/Will have a swollen foot within ten li." Such death became the *han* of Arirang hill over which the *minjung* had to crawl. Then, how amazing to find that the Korean *minjung* could dance in the Spirit when they encountered the Gospel of Jesus Christ!

Cosmic and Historical Divine-Human Participation

The paradigm of the third theology is that of a theology of the Spirit based on cosmic and historical divine-human participation which is sought for in the language and experience of people who crawl with God and dance in the Spirit. The third theology is not a kind of pneumatology but a hermeneutic of the Spirit. Divine-human participation is Spirit-spirit participation.[12] The divine Spirit is more inclusive than the notion of the Holy Spirit which was defined as the third person of the Trinity in the first theology. The divine Spirit cannot be contained in the Holy Scriptures just as the Word of God is more than the Bible. The divine Spirit is universally present in the cosmos as well as in history. The *modus operandi* of the divine Spirit is prevenient grace in all dimensions of life including inorganic and organic lives, human persons, culture, and religion.

The third theology is not merely a theology of culture, religion, and life but a proper Christian theology in the Korean and Asian context. The matrix of Korean theology of the Spirit as the third theology is the Korean *minjung*'s archetypal experience of the Gospel of Jesus Christ. The Gospel means the free grace of God given for all and in all who have no merit and wholly depend on the merit of Jesus Christ. This was indeed the Good News for the helpless and hopeless masses of Korean people. The Gospel is also the love of God shed abroad in our heart by the Holy Spirit so that our faith can work by love for sanctification and perfection. Here the evangelical divine-human participation could be effectively applied to the new creation of traditional religions of self-cultivation. But it must presuppose the redemptive grace of Jesus Christ who freely takes the form of

16

universal presence of the Spirit. The (universally present) Spirit-(self-cultivating) spirit participation is the cultural-linguistic matrix of Korean theology of the Spirit.

---

1) The divine-human participation is an expression used by Albert Outler in his introduction to the 1st volume of the critical edition of John Wesley's works.

2) Cf. David Ray Griffin, *God and Religion in the Postmodern World* (State University of New York, 1989).

3) Cf. Walbert Buehlmann, *The Coming of the Third Church* (Orbis, 1982).

4) Cf. The Documents of the JPIC World Convocation in Seoul (Seoul, 1990).

5) Cf. "Baar Statement," *Current Dialogue,* No. 18 (WCC, 1990, June).

6) Konrad Raiser, "The Ecumenical Community for Jubilee in a New World Order." Opening presentation at the 1995 Jubilee Convention, Seoul, Korea.

7) Charles Hartshorne, *The Divine Relativity: A Social Conception of God* (Yale University Press, 1978), p. 20.

8) Cf. Masao Abe, "Kenotic God and Dynamic Sunyata" in *The Emptying God,* Cobb & Ives, ed (Orbis, 1990).

9) Jaroslav Pelikan, *The Christian Tradition,* Vol. 2 (The University of Chicago Press, 1977), p. 133.

10) 10 li is about 4 kilometers.

11) Marilyn J. Legge, "Poetry and Soup," *In God's Image,* Vol. 14, No. 3, 1995, Autumn, p. 64.

12) The distinction between the Spirit as the divine spirit and the spirit as the human spirit is Paul Tillich's. Cf. *Systematic Theology,* Vol. 3 (The University of Chicago Press, 1976).

CHAPTER 2

The Matrix of Korean Theology of the Spirit

THE MOVEMENT OF the Holy Spirit in the early Korean church, which is the matrix of Korean theology of the Spirit, includes not only the Great Revival (1907-1910) but also the translation and propagation of the Bible (1893-1910) and the Korean Christians' independence and reform movement which started from the March 1st Movement (1919). It consists of three stages: first, the translation of the Bible by both missionaries and their Korean helpers and the propagation of the Bible by Korean colporteurs and Bible women; second, the internalization of biblical language and the formation of faith communities through the collective experience of repentance and of the Holy Spirit; third, Korean Christians' participation in the liberation of the Korean people through the education, the discipline, and the network of faith communities. We are going to illuminate the structure of the cosmic and historical divine-human participation in the light of the archetypical experience of the Gospel which appeared in the three stages of the Holy Spirit movement in the early Korean Christian church.

1. The Korean Bible and the Archetypical Experience of the Gospel

The significance of the translation of the Bible into Korean cannot be compared with that of the Reformer's translation of the Bible into German or English. The appearance of the Korean Bible caused a revolution in the history of Korean religions. No classics of Confucianism and Buddhism were translated into Korean and almost all Koreans suffered illiteracy. The early Korean Christians learned the Korean script while they read the Korean Bible. Through the *koinonia* of the saints who shared the Bible, they acquired communicative competence in socioethical discourse with

18

their fellow men and women.[1] The nationwide propagation of the Bible by the colporteurs and the Bible women broke the ground for new local faith communities all around Korea.

In East Asia the Buddhist classics were owned and read exclusively by the elite monks, and the lay Buddhists were the adherents of popular Buddhism amalgamated with Shamanism. The Confucian classics were also the properties of the literati class who considered Chinese characters the true script while they looked down on their own vernacular script which was used by women and common people to read short stories for entertainment. The Korean translation of the Bible helped the vast majority of people break away from ignorance and age-old bondage and seek autonomy and maturity. Such awakened and enlightened people were organized by the colporteurs and the Bible women into the faith community of common people unheard of in Korean history. The basic faith communities of the Bible Christians played the crucial role in the nation-wide non-governmental organization of Korean people over against Japanese imperialism.

The epoch-making Revival in 1907 was achieved by the *sakyunghoe* (Bible examining meeting), which was a collective Bible class combined with a prayer meeting. This meeting incorporated into the open community of faith the countless people who were excluded from the privileged Confucian or Buddhist communities that interpreted the traditional religious classics. The emergence of this unique Christian community of interpretation was the starting point for a universal community of love and justice open to all regardless of class, sex, and race. The Reformers fought against the privileged status of the Roman Catholic priests in the matter of biblical interpretation. The priesthood of all believers is closely connected with the principle of "sola scriptura. If it is no longer the ecclesial council that is privileged to interpret, a serious problem of the critical standard of interpreting the Bible arises. Over against arbitrary interpretations of the Bible, Calvin introduced the principle of the "inner witness of the Spirit" (Romans 8:15) for the legitimate interpretation of the Bible. The Word of God can not be appropriately understood by its readers unless their hearts are illuminated by the Holy Spirit. But here again a critical criterion for legitimate interpretation is missing. Virtually every reader of the Bible can claim that he has the inner witness of the Spirit. Then confusion will be endless. This might be a hermeneutical source of Protestant denominationalism. One of the remarkable aspects of early Korean Christianity was its collective reading and interpretation of the Bible. The Protestant emphasis on the centrality of the biblical message as well as the principle of the inner witness of the Spirit were also shared by the early Korean Christians. But the principle which remains formal in Protestantism became the material subject matter in their interpretation of the Bible.

The early Korean Christian community of interpretation of the Word did not stop short at the witnessing of the Spirit within an individual interpreter's spirit. Through their collective reading of the Bible not only their hearts were illuminated by the Spirit, but also they themselves participated in the salvific liberation of the Spirit witnessing together with their spirits that they were the children of God. It was in John Wesley's Methodist movement influenced by German pietism that the inner witness of the Spirit was first considered the assurance of faith given to some Christians. Wesley's initial enthusiasm for the assurance of faith can be understood in his encounter with the Reformation message of *sola fide*. The crucial distinction between the faith of a son and the faith of a slave made the young Wesley claim assurance of faith as the prerequisite for every true Christian. But later he revised this claim because of the danger of Moravian antinomianism. Since the Moravian-Methodist understanding of the inner witness had little to do with the interpretation of the Bible, the objective ground of faith could be neglected by the 'inwardness' of the witness.

The missionaries' report about the Great Revival in 1907 usually described the collective confession of sin and of the outpouring of the Holy Spirit. It is worthy to note that any open confession of sin was an alien practice for East Asians. Unless the early Korean Christians had encountered the Word of the Bible, it was not possible for them to be convicted of sin in front of God. The enormous sense of helplessness and hopelessness prevalent in their times might make the early Korean Christians spiritually poor so that they could become open to the message of the kingdom of God. Korea became a Japanese protectorate in 1905. And the resistance movement of the 'righteous army,' mainly consisting of Confucian scholars and peasants, grew to its peak in 1907. The American missionaries made the best use of this situation for the Revival. J. Z. Moore, Methodist missionary, wrote:

> The old Gospel of the cross and the blood, and the resurrection, now has become a free, full, and perfect salvation to multitudes and has taken literally hundreds of lazy, shiftless, and purposeless Koreans and turned them into very dynamos of evangelistic power.

In such contemptuous expressions as "lazy, shiftless, and purposeless Koreans" lies an image of the suffering people who had to crawl over the hill of Arirang. The missionaries who knew the threat of Japanese imperialism to the Korean people deliberately kept silent about political matters. Rather they intentionally led the angry souls of Koreans to have personal relationships with God. It was indeed reactionary and typical of colonialistic missions. Instead of conscientizing the Korean people to become an independent nation, most of the missionaries attacked the Koreans' dead ancestors and religious traditions as if they were idols and idolatry.

Despite the reactionary aspect of the Revival, we should not miss the point of the early Korean Christians' archetypical experience of the Gospel. Through reading the Gospels which the colporteurs and the Bible women distributed, the early Korean Christians encountered the compassionate heart of Jesus Christ. Jesus had compassion on a large crowd (*ochlos*) who were like sheep without a shepherd (Mark 6:34). The Korean *minjung* who were "lazy, shiftless, and purposeless" were like sheep without a shepherd. Using another metaphor, they were like orphans without parents. Through believing in Jesus Christ as the Son of God, they were adopted as the children of God. They became the "dynamos of evangelistic power." Unlike other East Asian nations such as China and Japan, Korea could become a very fertile land for evangelism because her people became historical orphans when she was colonialized by pagan Japan. It is no wonder that the missionaries expressed their sense of awe and amazement because they came to sow the seed of the Gospel but they reaped its harvest instead. According to the Gospel of Matthew, Jesus had compassion on the crowds who "were harassed and helpless, like sheep without a shepherd" (Matthew 9:36). Were there neither religious leaders nor political leaders in Jesus' time? In fact there were many Pharisees, Sadducees, and Romans. But the Jewish people were still harassed and helpless, like sheep without a shepherd. This might be the worst situation in the history of the Jewish nation, but Jesus said, "The harvest is plentiful" (Matthew 9:37). The human loss of the nation became a divine opportunity for the kingdom of God.

The scandal as well as the power of the Gospel in the early Korean mission was derived from the Father-Son relationship rooted in the Christian Bible. It is impossible in Confucian thought to think of God as the Father who has the Son. The father-son relationship was strictly confined to the most basic ethos of human relationships in Confucian ethics. In the eyes of Confucianists the Christian claim that Jesus is the Son of God "tends to undermine the significance of familial relationships."[3] The God of the Gospels should not be confused either with the wholly other who absolutely transcends the world or with heaven which is merely the transpersonal principle of cosmic harmony. But the dichotomy between the religion of grace and the religion of self-cultivation only exists in abstraction. The Christian doctrine of sin and grace was alien to Confucian tradition, but it was not so much a dogma as a living experience for the early Korean Christians. The personal, transcendent God, who was translated into *Hananim* in Korean, was not aloof and indifferent. On the contrary, God "so loved the world and gave His only Son" (John 3:16).

The surprising discovery of God the Father awakened the early Korean Christians to awareness of their adoption as the children of God. This awareness was given by the Holy Spirit's witness together with their own spirits in crying "*Abba*, Father!" The conversion story of Kil Sun-ju (1869-1935), the most prominent leader of the Great Revival, is a good example of the archetypical experience of the Gospel. When his Christian friend asked Kil to pray to God the Father, long-time Taoist Kil said, "How could man call God the Father?" Three days later, "while Kil was praying God to let him know that Jesus is the true savior,. . . .he heard a mysterious voice from above three times 'Kil Sun-juya, Kil Sun-juya, Kil Sun-juya!' He feared, trembled and could not raise up his head. Then he prostrated to pray and to cry out 'God the Father who loves me, forgive my sin and save my life.' His body became like a ball of fire and he continued to pray earnestly."[4]

The religious revolution that the Gospel brought about did not mean a mere substitution for Buddhism or Confucianism, but it rather meant a creative transformation of traditional religions without losing the essence of Gospel. And this happened not through any philosophical exchange but through the early Korean Christians' archetypical experience of biblical truth along with the witness of the Holy Spirit. The essence of the Gospel that God the Father gave us His only Son, so that whosoever believes will have the witness of the Spirit, was an enormous religious and cultural shock for Korean people saturated by Confucian tradition for more than five hundred years. The early Korean Christians' experience of God as the Father is not understandable without knowing the great significance of the work of the Spirit that made children of God out of such historical orphans. Through calling God the Father they challenged the age-old oppressive ties of familism, classism, and ageism because the arbitrary rule of many fathers of family, clan, and power structures was overthrown by the Gospel of Jesus Christ. According to Confucian tradition, one "could not bypass his social relationships in order to establish an intimate connection with Heaven directly."[5] This Confucian ideology of gradual development from

22

self-cultivation through family and state to world peace stops short at Confucian Pelagianism which can never imagine the grace of the heavenly Father for a breakthrough from above. The vast majority of the Korean minjung who were left out in the Confucian regime ironically became the subjects of history through encountering the religion of grace.

2. Collective Audible Prayer and the Formation of A Universal Community of Faith.

The missionaries' reports of the Great Revival described the early Korean Christians' experience of the Gospel in terms of "the out-pouring of the Holy Spirit," "the descending of the Spirit," "the coming of the Spirit," and "the infilling of the Holy Ghost." But this experience of the Spirit presupposes the powerful confession of sin. It may not be easy to understand that the people domesticated by religions of self-cultivation like Confucianism and Buddhism felt fear caused by their guilt in front of the transcendent God. The well-known prejudice that the guilt conscious-ness of an individual before God does not exist among East Asian people because of Confucian collectivism of family and clan can not be applied to the early Korean Christians. Their deep sense of helplessness and hopelessness in front of God sharpened their ethical consciousness. After Korea lost its diplomatic sovereignty in 1905, many patriots committed suicide and the uprising of the righteous army reached its peak in 1907. In this kind of situation it seemed reactionary to confess personal sin and to yearn for personal salvation. The missionaries reported the confessing of such personal sins as a husband's maltreatment of his wife, gambling and drunkenness, robbery and adultery, etc. What the missionaries will-ingly and unwillingly did not notice was the communal background of the early Christians" conversion experiences. Despite the missionaries' inten-tional effort to transfer the anger of Koreans who lost their nation to the consolation of a personal relationship with the Lord, we can still discern the signs of the crisis consciousness the early Korean Christians had in their collective experience of the Holy Spirit. There was a trace of taking their national crisis in as their own problem in the depth of their guilt conscious-ness. It was hidden in the so-called *tongsung* (collective audible) prayer which was an important trait of the Revival. The power of *tongsung* prayer, which filled even the missionaries with wonder and awe, dramati-cally expressed the groans of the Spirit of God present among the people crawling over the hill of suffering. G. S. McCune reported of "the Holy Spirit in Pyengyang:"

23

After Mr. Hunt's sermon Mr. Lee said a few words. The latter said "Let us pray," and immediately the room full of men was filled with voices lifted to God in prayer. I am sure that most of the men in the room were praying aloud. It was wonderful! No man prayed with a loud voice, and yet if you would listen, you could distinguish between the different ones. Some were crying and pleading God's forgiveness for certain sins which they named to Him in prayer. All were pleading for the infilling of the Holy Ghost. Although there were so many voices, there was no confusion at all. It was all a subdued, perfect harmony. I can not explain it with words. One must surely witness such to be able to understand it. There was an absence of the sensational, the 'emotional' (in the sense in which the word is so often used), and there was perfect concentration in the prayer of each one.

Collective audible prayer is the early Korean Christians' typical prayer. A superficial observer would miss the deeper unity of such prayer which looked as if it were a mere collection of individual prayers. Each and every praying person sighed, pleaded, and cried out before God in a deep sense of unity. It is not uniformity erasing individuality but unity affirming individuality. Such prayer neither robbed individuals of their community nor reduced individuals to uniformity. Instead it helped an individual keep his concentration without confusion and in perfect harmony with the community. *Tongsung* literally means the communication of voices. In *tongsung* prayer one's voice comes out of oneself while one hears the others' voices outside oneself so that a voice is in oneself and one is surrounded by many other voices at the same time. In this regard *tongsung* prayer is the prayer of the Holy Spirit. In *tongsung* prayer, to listen to the others' prayers is as important as to raise one's voice in his prayer because the Spirit precedes one's prayer in its intercession for him "with groans that words can not express" (Romans. 8:26).

There are many incidents of collective audible prayer in the Old Testament. The Hebrew people, when the Egyptians severely oppressed them, cried out to God (Exodus 3:7). And God called Moses to liberate them from Pharaoh's hands. There was no indication of open confession of sin in the Exodus story because their suffering was not considered the result of their sin. But there was the indication of sins when the Israelites cried out to the Lord under the slavery of Cushan-Rishathaim (Judges 3:7-9). The Israelites' sin against God was caused by their worship of the Baals and the Asherahs. Therefore, God punished them and they cried out to God. And God raised up a deliverer, Othniel. Here their crying out means their repentance. Then the Spirit of God came upon a deliverer of the Israelites. The repentance and forgiveness of sin as well as the coming of the Spirit upon their deliverer brought about a reconstruction of the

24

community of the people of God.[7] But the innumerable efforts for the reconstruction of community in the history of Israel failed to the point that God himself promised to cure them of backsliding (Jeremiah 3:22). In the New Testament the central event of Pentecost was not collective audible prayer but speaking in tongues. There was no painstaking process of repentance. But collective audible prayer rather than speaking in tongues might have been an authentic sign of the work of the Spirit reconstructing faith communities not only in the history of Israel and the early church but also in the history of the early Korean church.[8] It was Paul who first criticized the collective, public use of speaking in tongues (1 Cor.14: 19). It is far from the truth to suspect that Paul undermined public worship services led by the Holy Spirit. No one can understand Paul's doctrine of prayer and of the Spirit unless it is properly located in its original place, namely the Spirit-filled worshiping communities. Paul's thought of the witness of the Spirit was derived from his experience of the worshiping communities in which the early Christians did pray aloud together by crying "*Abba*, Father" (Romans 8:15).

According to Paul, the baptism of the Holy Spirit does not mean speaking in tongues. It rather means Christians "were all baptized by one Spirit into one body, whether Jews or Greeks, slaves or free" (1 Corinthians 12:13). It is why love is the most excellent gift of the Spirit and the community led by the Spirit is the universal community of faith. The early Korean Christian communities were literally the communities of both free and slave, of both man and woman, of both Westerner and Easterner. Park Sung-chun (1862-?), one of butchers who were considered the lowest class in traditional Korea, became a Christian in 1895. For him to become a Christian meant to become a human being.[9] In traditional Korea, butchers could not have jobs other than butchery. Their children had to become butchers and should marry the children of butchers. They were the outcasts of society and the scum of history. S. F. Moors, a missionary with love and courage, helped Park form the first community of other butcher Christians. Park later became a lay leader of his church along with another lay leader who belonged to the royal family.

3. The Holy Spirit Movement
and the Reform of Social Institutions

The Holy Spirit movement of the early Korean Christian church took place when the traditional Confucian regime was under total attack from both Japanese and Western imperialism. The colonial powers which threatened personal as well as national security shook the ground of the traditional communal ethos prevalent in Korean family life and social structure. In this anomic situation people sought a messianic hope from a new religious movement. From the very beginning of the Protestant mission in 1895 the missionaries and Korean Christians initiated progressive social movements which challenged both the reactionary party in Korean government and the foreign imperialistic powers. H. G. Appenzeller, the first Methodist missionary, built the first Methodist church and the first modern school in Korea. He also supported the prominent Korean Christian leaders Suh Jae-pil and Yun Chi-ho who organized and led the Independence Club, the first non-governmental civil organization in modern Korean history. It was a great loss for both the Korean church and the Korean people that Appenzeller died in an accident in 1902. He was an ideal type of missionary who combined the evangelistic conviction of the witness of the Spirit with the prophetic sensitivity of ecumenical praxis. After the tragic failure of the Independence Club, which attempted a gradual reform for constitutional monarchy in order to achieve its final goal of a democratic nation state, most of the missionaries were coopted by the colonialist policy of Marquis Ito, who abused the separation of church and state. Because the missionaries agreed with the ideological abuse of the separation of church and state and also because they were puppets of U. S. foreign policy, they cooperated with the Japanese in the name of freedom for mission. The Taft-Katsura agreement in 1905 was a secret agreement between the United States and Japan not to interfere with each other's imperialistic claims. Thus the United States kept silent about Japanese colonialization of Korea while the Philippines became a colony of the United Sytates with Japanese cooperation. The reactionary theology of mission that separated moral and spiritual enlightenment from social political engagement was established by hypocritical missionaries whose separation from politics in Korea was the outcome of their demonic endorsement of the Japan-U.S. secret international agreement.

The missionaries' and the Japanese imperialists' abuse of the separation of church and state suppressed the potential power of social reform within the messianic Holy Spirit movement of the early Korean Christian church. Nevertheless, the dynamic participation of the early Korean Christians in various social reforms and in the national independence movement must have had something to do with the historic formation of the universal community of faith, the only nationwide lay community challenging the Japanese. It is misleading to consider the Holy Spirit movement of the early Korean church merely the conversion movement of a colonialized people. A religious movement which does not bring about any institutional reform is nothing but a byproduct of social anomie. The Spirit of God can not be contained in the subjective spirits of human beings. It transforms all dimensions of human life including such objective spirits *qua* communities as family, civil society, and state. We cannot understand the genuine dynamics of the Korean theology of the Spirit unless we keenly perceive the relationship between the Holy Spirit movement of the early Korean church and reform movements on the various levels of Korean social institutions. Only when we can illuminate how the liberative praxis of communication was brought about by the Spirit in the various communities of Korean society, can we identify the true shape of the cosmic and historical divine-human participation which characterizes the matrix of the Korean theology of the Spirit.

1) Family Reform and Woman Liberation

In the record of a revival meeting in 1903 in Wonsan, we meet the first concrete penitent. According to Hardy's report, a young man repented of his sin with tears.[10] He was dispelled from an aristocratic family in Seoul and came to Wonsan to become a Christian. When he openly confessed his sin of fast living, especially of deserting his 19-year-old wife who was dying of sickness, all the members of the church wept. From then on this was the starting point for the open confession of sins. There were many cases of maltreatment of wives, adultery, and polygamy among the sins openly confessed by the early Korean Christians. In a patriarchal society such sins were committed by males without feeling the pangs of conscience. These are not merely personal sins but communal sins affecting the institution of marriage and family life. Usually in the afternoons during the Revival the Korean male and female Christians held open discussions of such themes as early marriage, education, sanitation, and smoking. These themes, which were connected with self-cultivation and family life, had been exclusively dealt with by the Confucian literati all of whom were males.

The progressive movement for the education of women and their equal status in the family was an important part of the Holy Spirit movement of the early Korean church. The very fact that the early Korean Christian women, who were educated in church-related schools, became the partners of men in their discussions of institutional reform and ethics demonstrates the work of the Spirit. Already in a Christian symposium held in 1897 a number of men and women participated in an earnest discussion concerning the equal treatment and education of man and woman. Some of the ladies were reported to claim that "Despite Eve's sinning, without Mary Jesus could not be born to the world to redeem our sin."[11] This statement reveals a new image of woman who was liberated from the age-old bondage of patriarchy which blames Eve for her sin, and who was identified with the poor servant girl Mary, chosen by the Spirit of God to become the mother of Jesus.

There were many Marys among the Bible women in the early Korean church. A Bible woman called Hannah in Hamheung, who was baptized by the Spirit during the Great Revival, sold 426 Gospels, and preached to more than three thousand women, and also taught a class of children in the Sunday school.[12] Her devout prayers and bright testimonies were so convincing that even the Korean men showed respect for her. And Sarah, a Bible woman in Suwon, taught little girls and women to read the Gospels and persuaded many women "to destroy the various things in their houses connected with the devil worship." Because of that it became an established custom to send for a Bible woman to pray with and for them when they were sick instead of sending for the Shaman.[13] It is significant to notice that sorceries were disenchanted by the prophetic ministry of the Bible women while the traditional priestly role of the Shaman was taken by the Bible woman. There were countless nameless Bible women who extended the Gospel to Korean women who were the *minjung* of the *minjung*. Through transforming them by the Gospel, the Bible women contributed to the reform of the family which is the basic unit of all social institutions.

The liberation of women in the colonial situation should not be confused with the feminist movement of the First World. Since the early Korean Christian women had to live in the suffering history of their nation, their woman liberation should not be based on bourgeois liberal individualism which became reactionary in the colonial context. This is the reason why their woman liberation from patriarchy should coincide with the liberation of their nation from colonialism. A prototype of such woman liberation coinciding with national liberation can be found in the life of Choi Yong-shin (1909-1935) who was a pioneer of the rural enlightenment drive in the 1930s. Her contemporary educated young women were exposed to the self-deceptive dream of sweet home which seduced them to surrender to the colonial reality as soon as they escaped the traditional bondage of patriarchalism. But Choi Yong-shin refused to surrender. Instead she, a seminary student, committed herself to the enlightenment of rural people. In the novel *Evergreen Tree*, which was based on her life of commitment and self-sacrifice, the heroine said to her mother, who wanted her daughter to marry a bank clerk:

> Of course, I am your daughter you bore and raised up. But I can not be only your daughter. Could you understand? I may be unfilial to you, yet I

have sacrificed this one body for the sake of the thousands or ten thousands of future mothers. . . . My work is a lot holier and more meaningful than letting my flesh dependent on Kim Jung-kun, isn't it? Mom![14]

The novel ended with her sudden death caused by overwork. In the last paragraph of the novel, her real lover and comrade, Park Dong-hyuk, coming back to his home village after burying her, walked toward the shade of the evergreen trees. Here the image of an evergreen tree represents the spirit of a nationalist which did not lose its 'greenness' despite the snow storms of oppression and persecution blown in the endless winter of suffering history. After Choi Yong-shin, this evergreen spirit has grasped and inspired countless young Korean intellectuals. One of the favorite songs sung in the 1980s by the Korean students struggling for the democratization and reunification of Korea is "Evergreen Tree":

Look! the evergreen tree in that plain / Nobody cares for it
Rainy wind blows, snow storm strikes / Still green, ever green till the end of the world

2) Social Reform and Nationalism

The great wave of the Gospel, spreading all over the nation, gave rise to the only nationwide popular organization under the Japanese regime. What made the Holy Spirit movement of the early Korean church fundamentally different from the North American revival movement in the nineteenth century was the fact that it went beyond the limit of individualistic conversion to incorporate the liberation movement of the colonialized nation. In 1919 the Korean Christians and the followers of Chundokyo, a native messianic religion, led the March 1st Independence Movement. It was a purely non-violent protest against Japanese colonialism, yet the Japanese killed almost 8,000 innocent Koreans, most of whom were Christians. Both Christian and Chundokyo leaders were affected by U. S. president Wilson's statement that the people of all nations should have the power of self-determination. Despite its naive utopianism, the vision of the March 1st Independence Declaration still remains one of the most viable options for peace and justice in East Asia:

The independence of Korea will make Koreans enjoy their just affluent life, and it will make Japan to avoid her evil direction so that she might take hold of the heavy responsibility to support Asia, and it will also make China escape her fear and anxiety from which she never dreamt of being free, and finally it will achieve peace in Asia which is the essential part of world peace and the necessary stage for the prosperity of humankind.[15]

This declaration is not one of ultra-nationalism but of self-transcending nationalism which contributes to international peace and justice. The spirit of the March 1st Declaration is partially succeeded by the Jubilee spirit of the 1988 Declaration of Peace and Reunification of Korea adopted by the NCCK. In the March 1st Declaration, the lack of realism concerning international politics is correlated with the absence of the open confession of sin. In this respect an unofficial statement taken by some Christian nationalists, "Appeal of Independence Party," represents the Jubilee spirit much better than the official declaration of the March 1st Movement:

> Dear respectful members of Independence Party! Do not insult Japanese on any occasion, do not throw stones at them or do not hit them by fists. Such are barbarous behaviors and will harm our claim of independence. Every believer should pray three times a day and should fast on Sunday. The everyday Bible readings are followings: Isa. 20 for Monday, Jer. 12 for Tuesday, Deut. 28 for Wednesday, James 5 for Thursday, Isa. 59 for Friday, Rom. 8 for Saturday.[16]

The above biblical guideline for the non-violent independence movement implies important theological insights. First, the destruction of the nation was caused by sin against God (Jeremiah 12; Deuteronomy 28). Second, Assyria, which destroyed Israel, would be punished by God (Isaiah 10). Third, Korean Christians have to repent of their national sin and take patience in their suffering (James 5; Isaiah 59). Fourth, the Spirit of God will intercede for Korean Christians, suffering for their nation, with groans that words can not express, and the glory of the future life can not be compared with the present sufferings. Besides the realistic outlook of international political situations, in which the superpowers oppressed the weak nations on the one hand and call for the confession of sin on the other, it also indicates the election of God preceding human knowledge of God. It means that God chose the suffering Korean people just as God chose Israel in spite of their sin. It also asserts that God took sides with the crawling people of both Korea and Israel and would judge the oppressive nations like Japan and Assyriya. It finally concludes that the Spirit of God witnesses with the spirits of God's chosen people that they are God's children. "For those

God foreknew he also predestined to be conformed to the likeness of his Son, that he might be the firstborn among many brothers. And those he predestined, he also called; those he called, he also justified; those he justified, he also glorified" (Romans 8:29-30). Indeed the early Korean Christians' archetypical experience of the Gospel, in terms of the witness of the Spirit, was grounded on the fundamental truth of divine election in the sense that they, the adopted children of God, are "predestined to be conformed to the likeness of his Son." Here divine election and conformity to the image of Christ are interdependent, another expression of divine-human participation.

Lee Seung-hun (1864-1930) was a Christian national leader and educator who authentically represents the early Korean Christians. He was born in a common family and did not receive any formal education, whether traditional or modern. He was a successful merchant until his middle age. After that he committed himself to the nationalistic education of Korean young people and became a Christian. When he was tortured by the Japanese police because of the Conspiracy case in 1911, he told himself that suffering was the necessary consequence of the Korean ancestors' disobedience to the will of God. He had a keen prophetic awareness in interpreting the historical sin committed by the brutal rulers and foolish people of Korea as an analogy to that of Israel. When some Korean pastors hesitated to take part in the March 1st Independence Movement because political engagement would violate the separation of church and state and because Christians' solidarity with the people of other faiths might cost the purity of Christian faith, Lee Seung-hun scolded them by saying "How can such a bastard without nation go up to heaven? All people except you are in hell, how will you rest in heaven and look down on them?"[17] For him, heaven and hell were not transcendent realms after life. His radical demythologization of heaven and hell made him discover a true heaven opened up in the very midst of a hellish world. His prison life witnessed how he endured the unbearable pain caused by the most inhuman torture and how he did live a heaven there. Whenever tortured, he prayed to be patient like Jesus on the cross. He completely obeyed the divine election to be conformed to the likeness of the Son. He could encounter the meaning and power of the cross of Christ in his prison life not because he escaped reality to soar up to a heavenly home but because he went down to the lowest hell to crawl with his people as well as with the Lord over the hill of Arirang. Lee Seung-hun volunteered to clean all honey buckets in the prison and from time to time cheerfully danced a spirited dance. Yes, he was a man who crawled with God and danced in the Spirit!

4. The Course the Holy Spirit Movement of the Korean Church Should Take in the Future

After the downfall of the premodern dynasty, the Korean people could not establish a modern nation-state because of Japanese-Western colonialism. Despite the pro-Japanese missionaries' policy and theology of the separation of church and state, for the sake of the mere survival of the Korean church, many early Korean Christians carried out progressive tasks on the various dimensions of social institutions such as family, education, culture, politics, and economy. Since the division of North and South, the Korean church has been so captivated by anticommunism and the capitalist system of market economy that she could achieve rapid numerical growth while ignoring the social mission of human rights, democracy, and peaceful reunification. Her present enthusiasm for overseas mission can hardly overcome a neocolonialistic missiology which is coopted by the Korean capitalist system operating in the mission fields. The Holy Spirit movement of the present Korean church, whether it be church growth or overseas mission, cannot help but become reactionary if it contradicts the universal values of human rights, democracy, and world peace. But the Holy Spirit movement of the early Korean Christians, whose archetypical experience of the Gospel made them work for cosmic and historical divine-human participation in various institutional reform drives, was progressive and decolonializing. The course the Holy Spirit movement is to take in the future has to start with retrieving the archetypical experience of the early Christians so that Korean Christians might lead the Jubilee mission of peace, justice, and the integrity of creation in Northeast Asia as well as in the divided Korea.

---

1) Cf. Juergen Habermas, *The Theory of Communicative Action,* Vol. 2 (Beacon Press, 1987); Edmund Arens, *Habermas und die Theologie* (Patmos, 1989).

2) J. Z. Moore, "The Great Revival Year," *The Korea Mission Field,* August, 1907, 118.

3) Tu Wei-Ming, *Confucian Thought* (State University of New York Press, 1991), 123.

4) Lee Deok-joo, *A Study on the Early Christian History in Korea* (The Institute for Korean Church History, 1995), 89.

5) Tu Wei-Ming, *op. cit.,* 127.

6) G. S. McCune, "The Holy Spirit in Pyengyang," *The Korea Mission Field,* January, 1907, 1.

7) Cf. Michael Welker, *Gottes Geist: Theologie des Heiligen Geistes* (Neukirchener Verlag, 1992), ch. 1.

8) Cf. Harvey Cox, *Fire From Heaven* (Addison-Wesley Publishing Company, 1995), ch. 11.

9) M. Hunley, *Caring, Growing, Changing: A History of the Protestant Mission in Korea*, 1904, 70.

10) R. A. Hardie, "R. A. Hardie's Report," *Minutes of the Annual Meetings of the Korea Mission of the Methodist Episcopal Church*, South, 1904, 24.

11) Lee Deok-joo, *op. cit.*, 64.

12) L. H. McCully, "Fruits of the Revival," *The Korea Mission Field*, June, 1907, 84.

13) Syster Isabel, "A Mutang's Conversion," *The Korea Mission Field*, June, 1907, 86.

14) Shim Hoon, *Evergreen Tree*, Contemporary Korean Literature 24 (Kemongsa Publishing Co., 1995), 155.

15) Choi Nam-sun, *Kimi Independence Declaration*, Contemporary Korean Literature 32 (Kemongsa Publishing Co., 1995), 50.

16) Lee Deok-joo, *op. cit.*, 240.

17) Lee Man-yul, *Korean Christianity and National Consciousness* (Chishik-sanupsa, 1991), 321.

CHAPTER 3

The Paradigm of Korean Theology of the Spirit

1. Mountain and Market, the Human and the Divine

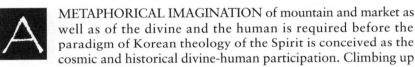METAPHORICAL IMAGINATION of mountain and market as well as of the divine and the human is required before the paradigm of Korean theology of the Spirit is conceived as the cosmic and historical divine-human participation. Climbing up and down a mountain must have begun in the earliest history of religions. The mountain was a holy place for the ancient who believed that gods descend to the mountain top. Whoever sought the divine went up to the mountain. Of course, there is a big difference between Judeo-Christian mountain climbing and Buddhist-Confucian mountain climbing. The theocentric motif of transforming history is predominant in the former and the pronature motif of self-cultivation is predominant in the latter. The two different styles of climbing gave birth to two different types of religion and culture.

The atmosphere of Christian monasteries, which look like fortresses, is almost hostile toward the surrounding mountains. Buddhist monasteries, placed in the midst of mountains like a baby in its mother's bosom, are open to the ecosystem of the mountains. Despite their openness toward nature they are relatively separated from the secular world, while Christian monasteries, especially in the Middle Age, used to be dynamically involved with the sociopolitical realm.

Chi-won, a ninth century Korean thinker, reported a deep and mysterious Tao in which Confucianism, Buddhism, and Taoism were integrated. He called it *pungryu*. *Pungryu,* which is literally "wind and flow" in Chinese, means to retreat from vulgar works to a scenic mountain and to play in good style. It refers to the classical Korean spirituality of those who cultivated themselves in the mountains full of cool wind and clean water.

34

Neo-Confucian scholar Lee Toe-gye went into a mountain after he resigned from the high office offered by his king. He built there a private Confucian institute to teach young people, to study Confucian classics and to enjoy *pungryu*. The slope of the mountain was used efficiently to make the ground for his institute. Behind it stood the range of mountains like a wall, and its facade faces a river within walking distance. Cool wind blows and clean water flows there. It is one of the best place for *pungryu* in Korea. Toe-gye, which means retreat to valley, rhymed his *pungryu* experience in the twelve poems which describe the deep, mysterious Tao of *pungryu* he enjoyed in the mountain. The fifth one says,

> Why green mountain is green for ten thousand years?
> Why flowing water never stops day and night?
> Let's not stop being green evermore.

The genre of the poem is *shijo*, which used to be popular among aristocrats as well as common people. The spontaneity of the mountain, the river, and the human being is well manifested in the poem. Toe-gye's *pungryu* aims at self-cultivation in harmony with green and clean nature in order to attain wisdom in human nature. His wish for being green evermore reflects an ecological view of life in the guise of neo-Confucianism. Toe-gye's green philosophy, which supports the nonduality of mind and body and of the divine and the human, is more commensurate with the biblical understanding of the Spirit than with Gnosticism.

The Spirit of God in Hebrew is *ruach,* which is the breath or wind of God. The *modus operandi* of the Creator God is the *pungryu* (wind and flow) of God the Spirit.

> In the beginning God created heaven and earth. Now the earth was a formless void, there was darkness over the deep, with a divine wind sweeping over the waters (Genesis 1: 1-2).

Creation began when the *ruach,* breath and wind of God, swept over the waters. Creation by the Word means God rhymed his *pungryu* experience. The universe was the poetic work of the playful God. God enjoyed his *pungryu,* so much that he exclaimed "So good!" at the end of every stanza of his poem. In God's *pungryu,* work and play are one, and the culmination of his playful creation is his creative play, i.e., rest on the seventh day. God enjoys every bit of his creation for every being in the world is God's partner in his *pungryu.* According to the second story of creation God blew the breath *(ruach)* of life into man's nostrils

(Genesis 2:7). This text has been abused by Western civilization to differentiate the human being from the rest of living creatures and to justify human domination and exploitation of nature. The *ruach* of God, in the first story of creation, hovered over the waters which were the womb of life and included all living beings. The breath of God in God himself, the breath of God in the human being, and the breath of God in the other living beings are the same *ruach* of God, the Spirit.

A religious leader who succeeded to Chi Chi-won's deep and mysterious Tao of *pungryu* was Chi Jeh-woo (1824-1864). Eastern learning was his religious thought as well as religious movement which attempted to integrate the challenge of Western Learning (Roman Catholicism) into the deep, mysterious Tao of Confucianism, Buddhism, and Taoism. Facing a double contradiction, i. e., the invasion of Western imperial powers and the corruption of the Confucian regime, Chi proclaimed the crawling *minjung* the imminent opening of the latter heaven. He taught that the latter heaven could dawn on them through the descending of the Spirit of God into the very body of each and every one of the groaning *minjung*. He was accused of disseminating Roman Catholicism and toppling the government. He was executed in 1864. After roaming over every corner of his world he settled down in his mountain village where he went though an enormous religious experience which became paradigmatic for his many followers. This paradigmatic experience was well manifested in his mantra which in turn provided for his followers the prototype of such an experience.

> Supreme *ki* being here and now
> I yearn for its great descent
>
> Waiting on Heavenly Lord
> My heart creatively evolves
> Let me never forget
> to communicate with every occurrence.

The first part of the mantra is an invocation *(epiklesis)* of the supreme *ki(Chi* in Korean). Well known in East Asia, *ki* is "a vital, dynamic, original power that permeates the entire universe, indeed, all things (macrocosmic and microcosmic), and leads to an ultimate unity." Chinese theologian Chang Chunshen translates the Spirit into *Chi* (*ki* in Chinese): "*Chi* or spirit belongs not only to the cosmic and natural life-world, but is also closely connected with the moral dimension of human life. And over and above all this, it serves as the mysterious bridge between God and the human person."[1]

The supreme *ki* refers to the *ki* of the heavenly Lord. In the neo-Confucian society of traditional Korea, the *ri* (*logos*) principle of form and the universal was predominant over the *ki* (spirit) process of dynamics and the particular, so that the *ki* (vital power) of the *minjung* severely suppressed turned into *han*.

The image of the great descent of the supreme *ki* like a giant waterfall is associated with that of *pungryu*. Deepening Toe-gye's *pungryu*, which is analogous to creation spirituality, Chi Jeh-woo's *pungryu* opened up a new sensibility of redemptive religion without falling into the pitfall of opposition between creation and new creation. While Toe-gye's emphasis on the priority of *ri* to *ki* legitimated the Confucian regime, Chi's paradigm of the nondual supreme *ki*, a partial succession and overcoming of Yul-gok's theory of the priority of *ki* to *ri*, provided a momentum for social reform. For Yul-gok, "the positive laws as the actual manifestation of the *li* (*ri* in Chinese) in social life must be subordinated to the people's life situation which is the concrete manifestation of the *Chi*."[2] Unlike Yul-gok, who maintained the clear cut distinction between *ri* and *ki*, Chi reduced such distinction to the one supreme *ki*. Because of the lack of such distinction, there was no logical ground for mediation between the universal and the concrete. This was the reason why there was neither belief in the Mediator nor a critical distinction between God and man in the later 'Humanity is heaven' doctrine of Eastern Learning.

"Waiting on Heavenly Lord, my heart creatively evolves" is the central part of the mantra. When the supreme *ki* of God comes into the human heart, it turns out to be Divine Spirit, which in turn liberates the *han* (repressed *ki*) of a downtrodden person, participating in the process of creative evolution and communicating with all living beings struggling to overcome the force of entropy. Chi interprets "Waiting on Heavenly Lord" as "Inside Divine Spirit, outside *ki* moves, each and every one should know he cannot do otherwise." This reflects an organic, ecological worldview according to which human life and all other lives in the entire universe are one and the same body. If everyone does otherwise, i.e., if "each one seek his own peace," this reflects an egocentric, mechanistic worldview according to which one's body is separated from other living beings.

Recently Kim Ji-ha asked for a cultural movement of new *pungryu* to overcome the spiritual crisis of Korean society in which powerlessness, corruption, and the loss of direction are prevalent. New *pungryu*, which integrates Christian tradition as well as Western philosophy and science into the deep, mysterious Tao of Confucianism, Buddhism, and Taoism,

37

aims at the human discovery of self, fellowship with neighbors, reconciliation with nature, peaceful reunification of Korea, and the creative renewal of East Asian wisdom. Starting from Chi Je-woo's idea that "I am one body with all companions of the whole world," new *pungryu* seeks a new humanism in which the individual, autonomous human being is one body with the ecosystem as well as with other human beings. According to this new humanism, the human being is woven into the world. The human being is the body which is a net of spiritual communication, and spirit moves in each hair and on every fingernail.[3] This new humanism calls for a paradigm of the "unitive *ki* of body and spirit." The unitive *ki* is a vital yet fuzzy power of life which can be defined neither by the dichotomy of body and soul nor by the dualism of matter and mind. The unitive *ki* of body and spirit is the presence of the supreme *ki* of God who is not a patriarchal despot transcending the world absolutely and relating himself to it externally, but an eternal, boundless, and maternal being embracing all beings in the world and relating herself to each and every being internally. The paradigm of Korean theology of the Spirit replaces the Gnostic paradigm, permeated with the illusion of transcendence like an angelic flight, with the paradigm of nondual supreme *ki*, based on the imagination of the *ruach* of God crawling over the waters.

The paradigm of nondual supreme *ki* is a paradigm by which one can understand the deep, mysterious Tao of the Spirit of God, which cannot be reduced into either matter or spirit. Overcoming the illusion of transcendence, which is separated from earthly life, the paradigm of nondual supreme *ki* seeks the imagination of a crawl which makes one lie flat on the ground, crawling over a curved surface of time, fast or slow, in every direction until one's body gets smeared with blood. Through such process of sincere life one achieves a holy existence beyond ordinary life.[4] Using an analogy of mountain climbing, this is not a spirituality of flight in which one climbs up the mountain to separate oneself from earthly life and to taste a sublime, heavenly ecstasy. It is rather the spirituality of a crawl in which one climbs down the mountain to crawl with the vulgar, dirty, and demon-possessed *minjung* on the ground of the market, transforming the market dominated by economic value into a holy city or sanctified market where life is valued.

2. Roaming Over Holy Mountain

Roaming over Holy Mountain, by Chi Byung-hun (1858-1927), describes a dialogue among four persons representing Confucianism, Buddhism, Taoism, and Christianity. The dialogue takes place at a spiritual pavilion on a holy mountain while they enjoy their *pungryu*. The name of each participant contains the meaning of ultimate reality according to each tradition. Jindo, a Confucian scholar, means 'true Tao'; Wonghak, a Buddhist monk, 'perfect enlightenment'; Backwoon, a Taoist mystic, 'white cloud'. The name of the young Christian participant, however, is Sinchunong, an albatross which floats on the water with an open beak until a fish jumps into it. When the Christian participant introduces himself to the other participants, Jindo laughs because the name does not bear dignity. Sinchunong, whose literal meaning is 'old man who believes in heaven', is a metaphor to differentiate the religion of grace from that of self-cultivation. The dichotomy between the religion of grace and the religion of self-cultivation makes interreligious dialogue impossible. Chi considered the four participants fellow-travelers on the way to the truth of the Gospel.

> How deep the ocean of nature as masters met one another!
> At spiritual pavilion they exchanged their hearts.
> Finally four friends returned to one place.
> The way to heaven was in the Gospel.[5]

They had dialogue through this exchange of their own hearts seeking true nature. *Simsung* (heart-nature) is the key term which is found in Confucianism, Buddhism, and Taoism. *Simsung* is the entrance gate to the truth of ultimate reality. The three religions of East Asia are the ways to cultivate *simsung*. *Sim* (heart) is not the human heart alone but the heart of heaven as well. *Sung* (nature) is not just human nature but the way of heaven too. *Simsung* is indeed the point of contact between the human being and ultimate reality. According to Mencius, "he who gives full realization to his heart understands his own nature, and he who understands his own nature knows heaven" (Mencius 7A: 1). Since the heart comes to us from heaven, it also leads us back to heaven. The heart is the reality as well as the symbol of the human being's unity with heaven.

The *simsung* motif in East Asian religions should not be misunderstood as the motif of the human's effort to save himself. The antinomian wing of Protestantism, which falls into the dichotomy between law and Gospel, tends to contrast the evangelical faith in grace with the legalistic belief of other religions in human good works. As John Wesley pointed out, Protestant orthodoxy lost the religion of Jesus in which the religion of the heart and the spirit of the law are one. Wesley, who rediscovered the heart language in Scripture, was influenced by Eastern Orthodox fathers. His favorite Eastern father, Macarius, considered the heart, the inner depth of the soul, to be the center of spiritual life. He affirmed the dignity, purity, and perfection of human nature in its original form. Macarius is not different from Mencius, who strongly affirmed the innate goodness of human nature. Following Macarius, Wesley described what the true Christian seeks: "What he continually labors to cultivate in himself and others is, the real life of God in heart and soul, that kingdom of God, which consists in righteousness, peace, and joy in the Holy Ghost."[6]

In "The Doctrine of Sins," the first theological essay written by a Korean Protestant, Chi described the original state of Adam and Eve in terms of the purity of their hearts. "Their hearts so pure they could see the heavenly Lord, how joyful and blessed!"[7] Chi identified "the pure in heart" (Matthew 5:8) with the one who loves God with all his heart, with all his soul. Chi translated "with all your heart, with all your soul (Deuteronomy 6:5) as "with all your *sim*, with all your *sung*." He used the *simsung* motif of East Asian religions to understand the profound unity of the religion of Jesus and the greatest commandment of the law. Actual human beings, according to Chi's essay, could not see God because their hearts lost their purity in the Fall. The *simsung* of human existence was entirely and universally corrupted by sin which is "the disease no doctor in the world can cure." The heart has become calloused by such disease. The recovery of original *simsung*, Chi's definition of salvation, requires first and foremost the awakening of the diseased heart. The one who is awakened of his sins is the one who 'is poor in heart-soul' (Matthew 5:3), who has 'the empty heart'. This awakening of heart is the first step in the process of salvation of which perfect sanctification is the telos.

It is a uniquely East Asian way in which Chi associated the image of the holy mountain with that of the Sermon on the Mount as well as that of Eden. The three masters of the three East Asian religions sought the spiritual pavilion on the holy mountain where they yearned to become a sage, a Buddha, and a hermit with supernatural powers. For Chi, however, the holy mountain is not only the paradise lost but also the mount in the heart where the living Jesus proclaims the message of the kingdom. In *Roaming over Holy Mountain* Chi wrote;

> The holy mountain is the body of the believer, and the spiritual pavilion the heart. Any one, cultivating himself in Confucianism, Buddhism, and Taoism, can become a disciple of faith if the Holy Spirit leads his heart to communicate with Christians.[8]

40

In the end of the book, Chi, an ex-Confucian scholar, confessed that the three masters and the Albatross are not four individuals but four living traditions in his spiritual pilgrimage. The book ends with Chi's remark that he woke up after a long, mysterious dream of roaming over the holy mountain. Thus his interreligious dialogue was the intrareligious dialogue of an East Asian Christian for whom other living faiths exist inside as well as outside. And his intrareligious dialogue is a Spirit-centered dialogue in which a sinner can find his salvation through fellowship with the Spirit. He defined salvation as the return to God the Father through "the fellowship with the Spirit" which is possible when one believes in the Savior.[9]

The Spirit is not merely the guide for such intrareligious dialogue but also the healer who makes the return to God the Father possible by moving the heart to believe in the free grace of God the Son. Through "the fellowship with the Spirit" we are assured of that fact that "the Spirit himself joins with our spirit to bear witness that we are children of God" (Romans 8: 16). Chi's vision of fellowship with the Spirit refers to the cosmic human-divine participation which he shares with Eastern Orthodox fathers. Unlike Macarius, whose Platonism made his theology otherworldly as well as ascetic, Chi still kept the indigenous tradition of *pungryu* which valued the cultivation of the body (the holy mountain) as much as that of the heart (the spiritual pavilion). In this sense Chi's spirituality is more biblical than that of Macarius.

3. Between the Holy Mountain and the Market Place

While roaming over the holy mountain in his sweet dream, Chi woke up. Did he come back to reality? Did he climb down the mountain to the historical reality where the *minjung* suffered and struggled? While Chi felt wonderful being at the top of the holy mountain, Lee Seung-hun, his contemporary, went down deep into the lowest hell of his times, the honey buckets of the prison. The images of the spiritual pavilion and of the holy mountain, reminding us of a high level dialogue among the religious elites, have to be critically revised in our time of ecological crisis and socioeconomic oppression.

First, the present world is no longer the holy mountain free from the plagues of pollution and war. There is no Garden of Eden other than the earth, the only garden we have to care for and honor. Forgetting the needs of our garden, our covetous greed takes the riches it provides and wastes its goodness. What we need to do to care for our garden and honor the earth is first of all to realize there is no holy and safe place separated from the rest of the world. Every being in our only holy garden shares the same life empowered by the same *ruach, ki,* and Spirit of God

> Life is a holy thing, life is a whole,
> linking each creature and blessing us all,
> making connections of body and soul.[10]

Second, there has appeared, especially in the West, a spiritual illusion that retreats to the holy mountain in various ways and under many names. Quite a number of Western intellectuals, sensitive to the Western spiritual drought but insensitive to the Eastern spiritual flood, blindly turned to the East. Their utilitarian cocktail spirituality, mixing Buddhism, Hinduism, Taoism, new science, astrology, dietetics, mesmerism, parapsychology, psychotherapy, and anything exotic and profitable, has nothing to do with the sublime Confucian, Buddhist, and Taoist ideal of the sage. Furthermore, it perpetuates an affluent leisure class through everything from meditation centers and ashrams to the pseudospirituality of mental tranquility, physical fitness, and all sorts of health mania. Such spirituality, uprooted from Asian soil, is nothing but an abuse of Asian spirituality because it endorses an indifferent attitude toward the poor in Asia.

We have to re-read Scripture using the paradigm of the nondual supreme *ki* in order to form a new spirituality that climbs down to the market place as well as climbing up the holy mountain. The narrative sequence of Exodus (Exodus 1–18), the most important biblical reference in the Third World theology of liberation, has been interpreted as if the Exodus were liberation once and for all. The Exodus was a powerful metaphor in the history of the Korean church struggling for national liberation from Japanese imperialism. Therefore, it is no wonder that the Korean church proclaimed the Jubilee in 1995, fifty years after Korea was liberated in 1945. The Jubilee text (Leviticus 25) is a part of the Sinai tradition. The Sinai tradition embodies the close relationship between God and the holy mountain. Mount Sinai was not only the abode of God but also the object of sacred pilgrimage.[11] The prophet Elijah went in pilgrimage to Sinai to rejuvenate his faith in God (I Kings 19:8). Most importantly, Sinai was the place of covenant-making between God and Israel. The covenant-making was accomplished by Moses' climbing the mountain seven times. Why does the immensity of the Sinai tradition, covering half of Exodus, Leviticus, and the first ten chapters of Numbers, sit like a granite block in the Pentateuch? Why was there the Sinai detour which made the Israelites wander around the wilderness for forty years? Why should they crawl over the wilderness after their being lifted "upon wings of eagles" (Exodus 19:4)? These puzzling questions can be answered when we properly interpret the significance of Moses' mountain climbing.

The motif of mountain climbing used to be ignored in the interpretation of covenant-making. Through the movement of Moses up and down Mount Sinai seven times, God made the covenant with Israel to be present in the tent of meeting. In this process Moses and God, or Israel and God, appear to be the two covenant partners. Mount Sinai itself is entirely left out of the understanding of the Sinai tradition. This seems ridiculous to Korean Christians who love to live in very mountainous country. It must seem ridiculous to anybody who is concerned about our garden, the earth. One has to notice that the relationship between God and the mountain, as well as the relationship between human beings and the mountain, exists prior to the covenant-making between God and human beings. Only when we acknowledge the holy mountain as the covenant field in which God and Israel met, can we overcome the anti-ecological worldview of the so-called covenant theology. The Old Testament witnesses that the one on the holy mountain not only lives in the presence of God but also lives in peace with the other living creatures:

> Lord, who can find a home in your tent,
> who can dwell on your holy mountain? (Psalm 15:1)
> Thus, before they call I shall answer,
> before they stop speaking I shall have heard.
> The wolf and the young lamb will feed together,
> the lion will eat hay like the ox,
> and dust be the serpent's food.
> No hurt, no harm will be done
> on all my holy mountain,
> Lord says (Isaiah 65:24-25).

The eschatological goal of climbing the holy mountain is to transform human history dominated by the law of the jungle into "the new heaven and earth" (Isaiah 65:17) where peace, justice, and the integrity of creation is revered.

Moses' mountain climbing was closely connected to the formation of a community around the tent of meeting under the mountain. The tradition of the tent of meeting was deeply rooted in the Aaronic priests' post-exilic vision of the community of the Torah. The arbitrary ritual and institution of temple worship during the Monarchy had imprisoned and frozen the living faith in God. The faith of the tent of meeting dynamically relates holy mountain climbing with crawling on the market ground. No wonder Jesus stood with Moses and Elijah on the mountain of transfiguration. All three of them met God on the holy mountain. All of them went down the mountain to the filthy ground of the marketplace to let God's people free. The faith of the tent of meeting without holy mountain climbing falls in the anti-ecological, oppressive temple religion, and holy mountain climbing without the faith of the tent of meeting falls victim to the Gnostic illusion of transcendence.

The codes of law in the Sinai tradition were not for liberation once and for all but for the permanent process of liberation as cosmic sanctification. The people around the tent of meeting, who already had experienced or heard of the Exodus, were exhorted by the laws of God to sanctify their daily life by facing corruption, pollution, and alienation. The laws embody the spirituality of the tent of meeting. It is the kind of spirituality that unifies holy worship in the tent of meeting (Leviticus 1–10) with the unpolluted life at the tent home (Leviticus 11–18) and seeks the sanctification of the market and the cosmos (Leviticus 19–27). The law of Sabbath does not stop at resting from labor to fulfill the end of creation. It also includes the sanctification of the broad range of worldly life such as care for the poor and the alien (Leviticus 19:9-10, 33-34), prohibition of exploiting labor and holding back wages (Leviticus 19:13), justice at the law court, and fair transactions in the market (Leviticus 19:35-36). The laws of the Sabbatical Year and Jubilee ask for sanctification of the land as well as of the history taking place in it. In the Sabbath Year the land has its sabbatical rest which is "a Sabbath for the Lord" (Leviticus 25:4). The law of the Jubilee year demands emancipating the slaves, clearing all debts, returning seized lands, and giving rest to overworked fields. The spirit of Jubilee is the spirit to protest against the reification and commercialization of human-nature relationships as well as of human-community relationships and to transform the market dominated by economic value into a sanctified market or a holy city where life is valued. Life throughout the holy years, along with life up and down the holy mountain, is life grounded in the holy space-time continuum of the Spirit.

Jesus did live a life attuned to the holy space-time continuum of the Spirit. From time to time Jesus "went up on a mountainside to pray" (Mark 6:46). His last mountain climbing for prayer took place on the Mount of Olives (Mark 14:26) which was also the place of his Ascension (Acts 1:9).

44

For Jesus, holy mountain climbing and the cosmic sanctification of the market were closely related. His healing and exorcism were unthinkable without presupposing his prayer on the mountain sides. His holy mountain climbing filled him with the powerful Spirit of God. His healing and exorcism, the ministry of the Spirit, were the signs of the coming Kingdom of God. Jesus' mountain climbing and his messianic proclamation of "a year of favor from the Lord" (Luke 4:19) were in constant back-and-forth movement led by the holy space-time continuum of the Spirit. He climbed up the mountain of transfiguration to experience the peak of religious ecstasy (Luke 9:29), but he did not stay there. Instead, he climbed down it to "the place called the Skull" (Luke 23:33). Jesus' journey to Jerusalem to be crucified began right after his peak experience.

Jesus' last mountain climbing ended up with his arrest on the Mount of Olives. Climbing up the mountain voluntarily, Jesus could not climb down it by himself for he was caught by the forces of darkness. Jesus' last mountain climbing and his journey to Jerusalem were reenacted in Acts 1. Jesus' disciples climbed up the Mount of Olives, and the ascending Jesus said to them:

> You will receive the power of the Holy Spirit which will come on you, and you will be my witness not only in Jerusalem but throughout Judea and Samaria, and indeed to earth's remotest end (Acts 1:8).

Then, Jesus' disciples went back to Jerusalem to be filled with the Holy Spirit. It has to be remembered that Jesus' disciples also faced persecution and death despite their initial success in evangelism. The above passage should not be interpreted to mean the linear development of Christian mission. It must be rather understood in terms of the holy space-time continuum of the Spirit. Not simply Pentecost but Jesus' mountain climbing and his journey to the cross ought to be permanently reenacted by the church. Without Ascension, no Pentecost!

---

1) Hans Keung and Julia Ching, *Christianity and Chinese Religions* (New York: Doubleday, 1989), 266.

2) Kim Kyoung-jae, *Christianity and the encounter of Asian Religions* (Boekencentrum, 1994), 90.

3) Kim Ji-ha, "Northeastern community of life and new creation of culture", *Dialogue*, 1995, Summer, 41.

4) *Ibid.*, 125.

5) Choi Byung-hun, "Roaming over holy mountain", Ocksung Cha, ed., *Historical Resources of Korean Christianity*, vol. 1 (Korean Institute of Religion and Society, 1993), 80.

6) John Wesley, A Christian Library, *vol. 1 (London: T. Cordeux, 1819), 71.*
7) Cf. Choi Byung-hun, "Doctrine of sin", *Theological Monthly,* I-11, 446-455.
8) Choi Byung-hun *Roaming over holy mountain,* 108.
9) Cf. Choi Byung-hun, "Doctrine of sin".
10) "Honour the Earth", *Sound the Bamboo: CCA Hymnal 1990,* no. 269.
11) John J. Hayes, *Introduction to the Bible* (The Westminster Press), 71.

CHAPTER 4

Theology of the Spirit and Theology of Culture

1. Korean Theology of Indigenization and the Problem of Culture

THE THEME OF Christ and Korean culture has been the favorite theme of the so-called theologians of indigenization. For them the indigenization of the Gospel in Korean culture is not an artificial, scholarly work but the work of the Holy Spirit in the life of Korean Christians who receive the Gospel. As a model of contextual theology, Korean theology of indigenization is based on the fundamental thesis that the Spirit of God has already been effective in the history of the Korean spirit. Almost all of the Protestant theologians of indigenization are Methodist Koreans, who claim that the prevenient grace of God has guided the history of Korean religions toward the *kairos* of Jesus Christ.[1] The very term indigenization implies both the normativeness of the Gospel and the variability of the Korean cultural context; i.e., the Gospel is the substance of Korean culture and Korean culture is the form of the Gospel.[2] Thus the task of Korean theology is to correlate the Christian answer implied in the Gospel with the religious question implied in Korean culture. One thing the theologians of indigenization do not notice is that Korean people, who have lived with the highly developed religions of Asia, do not ask the questions to which the Gospel gives the answer. Unless one understands the indigenous form of the religious answer, even the best effort at indigenization imposes a foreign form of the Christian answer on Koreans. Since there is no pure Gospel devoid of a particular culture, it is absurd to correlate the Gospel with a local culture. Even the very form of the Gospels reflects certain cultural traits of the Jewish and Greco-Roman environments. Therefore, it is an idealistic understanding of culture to

47

presume that every culture seeks the same ultimate reality disguised in various forms.

The problem of an idealistic understanding of culture lies in the too easy equation of the religious symbols of ultimate reality in the two different cultural traditions. They are not two different cultural expressions of the same ultimate reality. They are rather two different cultural-linguistic systems which share almost nothing in common.[3] When the Bible was translated into Korean, the word God was translated as *Hanunim*. *Hanunim* was the term designating the supreme God in the Shamanistic pantheou. Belief in *Hanunim* is not so much monotheistic as henotheistic. In reality, as well as in the most well known *Tangun* myth, *Hanunim* stands aloof while the lesser gods are the actual deities affecting the lives of people.[4] *Han* or *khan* (in the Mongolian language) means the Grand One, Great, Ruler, King, and the Lord. *Nim* is a word used for honorific personification. But it is misleading to equate this *Hanunim* with the God of the Bible. Instead it is the biblical notion of God that gave the indigenous term *Hanunim* such monotheistic connotations. In other words, *Hanunim* and the God of the Bible are not two different expressions of the same ultimate reality because they come from culturally and linguistically different traditions. Belief in *Hanunim* was used by kings to sanction and solidify their regime. In this sense, the *Tangun* myth is nothing but the ideology of domination legitimizing the political power of ancient Korean rulers. As the Chinese emperors were the sole sons of the Heavenly Lord, the Korean kings were the only official worshippers of *Hanunim*. The common people were not allowed to worship *Hanunim*. Instead they worshipped the lesser gods of mountains, seas, and ancestors. It was indeed revolutionary in the history of Korean religions that the common Koreans could believe in *Hanunim*.

2. *Aunt Suni:* An Ensemble of Texts

There is no short cut in doing theology of indigenization. We must take a detour to understand the presence and work of the Spirit of God by interpreting the complex structure of Korean culture at the end of the twentieth century. The complex cultural system of present day Korea refers to the religion, customs, rituals, traditions, technology, thought, ideology, politics, and economy in and through which contemporary Koreans commonly live and express themselves. Let's start with a text in which the Confucianist, Shamanistic tradition and ideological, sociopolitical conflict are intertwined. The text is a particular story of a particular region, yet it embodies the common experience and the common language of contemporary Koreans. It is "Aunt Suni," a short story written by Hyun Ki-yúng who comes from beautiful Cheju island. His story is about the tragic massacre which took place in Cheju island on April 3 in 1948. Three years after the United States and the USSR divided Korea in 1945, pro-American leader Rhee Seung-man attempted to establish the South Korean government. Most of the Cheju people disagreed with the attempt and avoided the general election. When several hundred communist partisans rioted against the government, the South Korean soldiers killed several hundred thousand innocent people on Cheju island. "I," the protagonist in the story, who lived in Seoul in the 1970s, was a nephew of Aunt Suni. He visited his home village in Cheju island after having left there eight years before. The purpose of his visit was to participate in his grandfather's memorial rite. His grandfather was one of the victims of the April 3rd incident. The following text is part of the protagonist's recollection of his youthful experience of hearing the cries during the memorial rituals of several hundred families who lost their beloved ones at the same time on the same day.

Having headache caused by many confused ideas, I leaned my head backward on the wall and closed my eyes. Since I still felt uncomfortable, I dared to lie down behind Kilsu my cousin in front of the wall. The cold wind blowing through the open window cooled down the heat of my forehead. From time to time the strong wind scattered the small pellets of dry snow on the paper window. It sounded eerie as if a cat scratched the window by its front legs. Why was there so much of graupel in my home village? Was it caused by the windy weather? No. To the people of my village who used to eat sweet potatoes and millet, the graupel might look like glutinous rice. Only on the say of memorial rite could we eat *kon* rice. Why was it called kon rice? Is it because kon rice means fine rice which brightly shines? During my childhood I and Kilsu used to lie down to sleep curled up behind the back of the adult members of family in order to taste a couple of spoons of rice after the rite. On a pine board with strong resin odor which was used on behalf of the sacrificial table burnt up during the April 3rd incident, there was always a bowl of kon rice although they were financially unable to offer any thing fancy besides a dry fish, a shallow round plate of buckwheat jelly, a dish of cooked bracken and a dish of sliced and cooked radish. After the midnight when my eldest uncle woke up and pushed our backs to wash our faces, we went out to the frontyard to see the white graupel spread all over it. Then, the ominous wailing started from this house to that house, while dogs' barking ascending into sky. At the same time on the same day memorial rites began from this house to that house. The memorial rite of my grandfather used to start with the cry of my aunt, my father's sister. Next to the

49

cry of my 'big mother' (wife of my father's eldest brother) who came out of the kitchen, the wife of the cousin of my father began to cry. Ah, the wailing that bursted out from this house to that house at the same time and on the same day! On January eighteen according to lunar calendar, the whole village was full of the noise of specially prepared pigs hung on japonicas during daytime and the sad cries bursted out around the midnight when more than five hundred ghosts came down to eat rice. But we the more children used to pick up from the many corners of our village the urinal tubs of the dead pigs, and endured the terrible smell to blow them up fully through the stars and elatedly kicked them as if they were soccer balls. We were appalled by the unbearable wailing at midnight. While waiting for the rite, we abhorred to listen to the miserable stories of the April 3rd incident. We heard of the story so often that we were sick and tired of it. Why did the adults keep telling such tragic story to the mere children like us.[5]

This story is not a memoir of the memorial rite of ancestors which is frequently found in Korean society. Up until now the majority of Koreans have performed the rite in Confucian style on the day their parents pass away. In Korean society the memorial rite is a form of social interaction as well as a religious-cultural system of meaning. Every ordinary Korean, if he is not a Christian, knows how to behave on the day of a memorial rite. The issue of the memorial rite has become the dividing line between Christian (especially Protestant) Koreans and other Koreans. Thus to become a Christian has meant tension and even conflict with the rest of the family who perform the Confucianist memorial rite. The artificially invented Christian memorial service has nothing to do with the traditional memorial rite.

The story "Aunt Suni" does not show us the ordinary state of a family community gathering for the memorial rite. Instead it utilizes the motif of the memorial rite to introduce a neurotic Aunt Suni and to indict those who forget the tragic history of the Massacre caused by ideological division. Aunt Suni, a distant relative of the protagonist, lost her two sons in the April 3rd incident. Aunt Suni once came up to Seoul to stay at the protagonist's house for a while, but her Cheju accent and the fastidiousness caused by her neurosis made her a burden to the urban life of the protagonist's family. Aunt Suni's psyche was deeply hurt by the April 3rd incident. Many corpses were buried in her hollowed field. Whenever she weeded her field, she had an auditory hallucination of the gun fire and of the desperate cries of the massacred. The protagonist heard of her suicide when he returned to his village to participate in the memorial rite of his grandfather who was also murdered during the incident. Here his homecoming is not simply a return to the community for the memorial rite. It is rather a process of recovering the memory of the repressed *han* of those persons who were victimized by injustice in the April 3rd incident, indicting the current absence of healing and reconciliation.

Indeed, the protagonist's recovery of the critical memory of the Cheju massacre coincides with his return to the community for the memorial rite. And his memory of the memorial rite in his childhood becomes a clue helping him to participate in the rite anew. The victims and witnesses of the incident, the protagonist's relatives, gathered at the rite for his grand-father to 'tradition' the history of the massacre so that they themselves, as well as their descendants, may not forget it. Listening to the wailing bursting forth from several hundred families in the same night, they participated in the rite consoling the *han*-ridden souls of those victimized by the evil spirits dominating the era of division. In the story, the traditional meaning of the memorial rite is concretely applied and critically appropri-ated to disclose the tragic reality of the divided nation. Thus the configu-ration of Korean culture disclosed in such a story as "Aunt Suni" lies in an "ensemble of texts"[6] in which the Confucianist and Shamanistic tradition is intertwined with the disintegration of the local communities of blood ties caused by rapid modernization and cold-war ideology. There is no such a thing as a pure Confucianism, a pure Shamanism, or a pure Christianity which transcends the concrete sociopolitical reality of Korean history. And it is not a sort of religious, cultural syncretism of Confucian-ism, Shamanism, and Christianity that represents contemporary Korean culture. It is an old paradigm to believe that the indigenization of the Gospel is taking place in the religious, cultural realm distinguished from the political, economic realm. Korean culture is rather an ensemble of texts in which religion, politics, economy, technology, science, art, thoughts, ideologies, etc., make up a complex system. The task of a theology of culture is to understand this complex ensemble of texts.

3. The Spirit, the Healer of Culture

Writing of a theological semantics of culture in the Asian context, C. S. Song criticizes previous theologies of indigenization, inculturation and contextualization;

> Even the recent effort on the part of some theologians both in the East and in the West to 'indigenize,' 'acculturate,' or 'inculturate,' in a word, to 'contexualize' the Gospel in different cultures seems beside the point. The crux of the matter is not for the Christian Gospel 'to take roots' (indigenize)

in a culture unrelated historically to Christianity, 'to be adapted' (accultur-
ated) to a culture different from a culture shaped by the Christian faith, 'to
be interrelated' (inculturated) with a culture that shares little in common
with what the Christian church teaches and believes. All these efforts,
however laudable, presupposes that the culture that represents Christianity
is the norm by which other cultures are to be evaluated and changed. Implicit
in this approach is the transformation model--the Gospel transforming
cultures.[7]

A genuine theological semantics of culture helps Christian theologians
ask what a culture means for the people who live in that culture. The
primary task of a theology of culture is "to identify a culture's capacity for
self-purging and to explore how it works to sustain the life of people."[8]
This attitude contradicts that of infusing the transforming power of Christ
into a culture. We encounter the power of the Spirit creating and re-creating
a people and their community in that self-purging capacity. The self-purging capacity of culture is not so much self-healing as Spirit-healing. How
does the self-purging capacity of culture as the Spirit-healing of culture
appear in the story "Aunt Suni"? In such a context, what is the power of
healing which affects the conscience of those working for the renewal of
human relationships as well as for the transformation of society? It is found
neither in the mere return to the community for the memorial rite based
on the ethos of filial piety nor in the direct proclamation of salvation in
Christ. Without recognizing the serious challenge which comes from the
story, ending with a clear indictment and a prophetic critique of the
incompleteness of healing and reconciliation, it could be misleading to
claim that the final reconciliation, which heals the history of suffering, is
completed in Christ. This is true not because one can ignore the healing
and salvation by Christ, but because such insensitivity toward other
cultures keeps silent about the universal presence and work of the Spirit.
Out of such insensitivity have come antisemitism, the crusades, and
Christian imperialism.

Unlike the model of Christ as the transformer of culture, the model of
the Spirit as the healer of culture acknowledges the self-purging capacity
of culture as the healing power of the Spirit within the participants in the
culture. The model of the Spirit as the healer of culture is already found in
the story form of Jesus' healing miracles, especially in the Gospel of Mark.
The cultural-theological form of the Gospel of Mark is that of an aretalogy,
namely, a biographical story form of a divine man who taught great
wisdom and performed miracles and suffered martyrdom.[9] The aretalogical form of the Gospel of Mark was intentionally used to witness to the

presence and work of the Spirit of Jesus Christ in the Hellenistic world. Especially the stories of Jesus' healings were introduced to the Hellenistic audience in the aretalogical form familiar to them so that the message of Jesus' healing and saving work within their culture could be persuasively proclaimed.

> Now there was a woman who had suffered from a hemorrhage for twelve years; after long and painful treatment under various doctors, she had spent all she had without being any the better for it; in fact, she was getting worse. She had heard about Jesus, and she came up through the crowd and touched his cloak from behind, thinking "If I can just touch his clothes, I shall be saved." And at once the source of the bleeding dried up, and she felt in herself that she was cured of her complaint. And at once aware of the power that had gone out from him, Jesus turned round in the crowd and said, "Who touched my clothes?" His disciples said to him, "You see how the crowd is pressing round you; how can you ask, 'Who touched me?'" But he continued to look round to see who had done it. Then the woman came forward, frightened and trembling because she knew what had happened to her, and she fell at his feet and told him the whole truth. "My daughter," he said, "your faith has restored you to health; go in peace and be free of your complaint" (Mark 5:25-34).

The healing of the bleeding woman was identified with her salvation. Here salvation meant the restitution of her rights and the restoration of lost human relations. Her sickness was considered anti-social because it was contrary to the holiness code of temple religion. She lost all her rights and responsibilities in her society. That was why she had to exist anonymously in the crowd and to approach Jesus in secret. Her sickness was not a mere disease in her body. It was rather the death of her identity as a person, the death of the meaning of her life, and the loss of her social place or belongingness. Therefore, her healing was her resurrection from these deaths. It is significant to note that she and Jesus at once were aware of her healing by the power of the Spirit. The *ki, ruach,* Spirit of God flew from Jesus to the woman. Nevertheless, Jesus said to her, "My daughter, your faith restored you to health, go in peace." Wasn't it a typical event of divine-human participation that Jesus healed and saved the woman? She was called a daughter of God by Jesus because she was not a non-subject of history any more. One of the most impressive aspects in the story is the active approach of a daughter of God toward Jesus, the Son of God. Korean *minjung* theologian Ahn Byung-mu criticizes most Western theologians' apologetical interpretation of the text, namely, that the story is a medium to reveal Jesus as the Christ. Instead, Ahn claims that most of the miracle stories in the Gospel of Mark are the reports of *minjung* *(ochlos)* events in which a rather timid Jesus could not help but heal the sick because he was surrounded by the strong demand of the passionate *minjung.*[10] The Christ event and the *minjung* event, however, are not in mutual conflict. They are united in the one great event of divine-human participation for the healing and salvation of *minjung.* The connectedness of the Spirit between the woman and Jesus should be understood from the perspective of such divine-human participation. And the above text and the whole aretalogical framework of the Passion and Resurrection narrative in the Gospel of Mark consist of a hermeneutical circle. The Spirit of the crucified and resurrected Jesus was the Spirit that healed, saved, and liberated the woman. Just as the woman was deserted by her family and society, Jesus was betrayed by his disciples and followers. Just as the story of the bleeding woman indicted the powerlessness of the various doctors, the Passion narrative of Jesus indicted the hypocrisy of Jewish leaders. Just as the healing of the woman was the restitution of her rights and the restoration of broken relationships, the resurrection of the crucified Jesus was God's vindication of the cause of Jesus' proclamation of the kingdom. The way that the woman touched Jesus' clothes is a metaphorical clue to understanding the model of the Spirit, the healer of culture. Thus her healing represents the healing of the culture to which she belonged.

4. Servant Community of the Spirit Ministering to the Living and the Dead

The following text is the story about a Shamanistic ritual for the healing of a person whose sickness was related to the April 3rd incident:

Mizo, a twenty-five year old Cheju *simbang* (Shamaness), told me the story of a man for whom she conducted a healing seance. The night before she was approached by the man's aunt, she had had a strange dream. In the dream she saw a young couple, wearing white clothes--clothes of mourning--whose mouths and chests were pierced by bamboo spears and whose wounds gushed blood. Early the next morning a middle-aged woman, Suni, came and asked Mizo to perform an urgent rite of exorcism for her nephew, who was in a life and death situation at a local hospital. For several years, he had suffered from gasping and a feeling of suffocation in his chest. Suspecting a connection with Suni's case, Mizo related her dream. With alarm and trepidation, Suni revealed that her nephew's parents had been killed with a bamboo spear and a gun during the April Third Event. This event was never spoken of. Yet Mizo's dream confirmed Suni's memory.

Mizo then suggested that a special rite, *chilchim*, for clearing the passage of the dead into the other world, be offered. Later that day Mizo started a *kut*--a Shamnanic ritual--at Suni's house. Suni's nephew, weak and bedridden, was brought in relatives' arms to the *kut*. During *yonggye-ullim*--a segment of the seance in which the dead lament through their spirit mediums, in this case Mizo--the ill man wept as his dead parents told the stories of their death and their sorrow at being unable to enter heaven because they had never received the rite clearing the passage to the other world. After the seance, Suni's nephew did not die, yet he remained sickly.[11]

On Cheju Island, whenever Shamanesses performed *kut* which was related to the April 3rd incident, they were under police surveillance. Since the incident was not fully uncovered, the person whose fatal sickness was related with the incident could not be healed by any *kut*. While the Confucianist memorial rite which has won social recognition is carried out by males, the Shamanistic rite which complements the Confucianist rite is carried out by women. These two rites are not a bisexual dual structure of faith. Instead they make up a complete system of popular faith in Korea.[12] Though the rites for the dead in Korea are mostly Confucianized, the Shamanistic *kut* is still alive because there must be some function which the Confucianist rite cannot fulfill. That missing function is *yonggye-ullim*, a segment of the seance in which the dead lament through their spirit mediums. The Confucianist rite, in which the ethos of filial piety is fundamental, produces the solidarity and continuity of the family unit. The Confucianist ideology of ancestor worship has sustained and consolidated Korean patriarchal social systems. Of course it is naive to assume that the Confucianist rite is merely a social custom, not a religion.[13] It also has a religious dimension, namely, its ceremony of calling the spirit.[14] Nevertheless, the Confucianist rite does not have the function of a spiritual medium as the Shamanistic rite *yonggye-ullim* does.

As shown above, both the Confucianist community of memorial rite in "Aunt Suni" and the Shamanistic community of Mizo and Suni (a different person of the same name) have the prophetic function of indictment against the murderers in the April 3rd incident. And both communities also have the priestly or ministerial function of consoling the victims and their families. What about the Christian community in Korea? Hasn't it kept its spirituality in a superior position over both the Confucianist and the Shamanistic communities? Hasn't it accused the Confucianist community of ancestor idolatry and the Shamanistic community of pagan necromancy? Then how can it serve and minister to those communities historically related to the April 3rd incident? For the same theological reasons mentioned above, will it abandon its ministry of justice, peace, and joy? If indeed ministry is the function of community, how does the Christian community relate itself to other communities to fulfill its ministry? To what extent can the Christian community in Korea be open to the Spiritual Presence in non-Christian communities? In order to answer these questions we have to understand the original form of the Christian community of the Eucharist in the Gospel of Mark.

It is significant to note that Jesus' institution of the Eucharist (Mark 14:22–25) is followed by the Passion narrative (Mark 14:27–15:47) which, in turn, is followed by the story of Jesus' Resurrection (Mark 16:1-8). This means that the Eucharist is the Christian rite of Passion and Resurrection. The Passion narrative is preceded by a certain sequence in Jesus' conflict with the Jewish leaders, i.e., the story of the withered fig tree (Mark 11), the parable of the wicked tenants (Mark 12), and the eschatological discourse (Mark 13). This sequence reports that Jesus' death was caused by his conflict with the Jewish authorities who tried to imprison and freeze Jesus' message of the kingdom of God. It also implies that the oral tradition of the Passion narrative grew out of the 'dangerous memory' of Jesus mortified and killed by the religious political leaders.[15] The community of the Eucharist was the very place where this dangerous memory was vivified and revivified by telling and retelling the Passion narrative. Through the constant sharing of the Eucharistic meal, the community confirmed and reconfirmed their solidarity with the crucified Jesus. The community of the Eucharist has the Resurrection narrative as well as the Passion narrative. The Resurrection as the once-and-for-all act of God for the crucified Jesus was the vindication of the legitimacy of Jesus' proclamation of the kingdom of God. It was also the sign of the coming of the living Spirit of Jesus to those who suffered injustice as the risen Jesus promised to go to Galilee. The message of the Resurrection--"He is risen!"--made the Eucharist, the Christian rite of the crucified, dead, and buried Jesus, the revolution of cultural and political rites for the dead. In other words, the focus of the Eucharist, which lies in the coming of the living Spirit of the dead and risen Lord, gives the Christian community the spiritual power to discern the *han*-ridden spirits of the victimized from the demonic spirits of the victimizers. This point is crucial in the cultural, political context of contemporary East Asia. Japan's largest Liberal Democratic Party recently adopted a party platform calling for cabinet members to visit Yasukuni Shrine that consecrates the Japanese war dead since the nineteenth century, including the executed war criminals of World War II. This is Japan's right-wing abuse of Japanese traditional reverence for the dead, signaling the resurgence of ultranationalism or imperialism as a general feature of the Japanese national psyche. It is not a handful of the spirits of the Japanese war criminals but the more than twenty thousand Korean and other Asian women in the Japanese prostitution army during World War II, used and torn by violence-hungry soldiers, who must be the genuine witnesses of the Resurrection in our times.[16] Despite their unbearable shame and suffering, a few Korean survivors among them faced the problem and courageously indicted the unrepentant Japanese of inhuman sins. How could they have the courage to stand up for justice and peace? Weren't they led by the living Spirit of the Resurrection? Over against the resurgence of the specter of Japanese militarism they have been witnessing to God's raising of their fellow victims' spirits from the dead. After all, wasn't it also women who first witnessed the Resurrection of the crucified, dead, and buried Jesus? Yes, the women of the earliest Christian community around the Eucharist table were the ones who overturned the patriarchal tradition of the Jewish sacrificial ceremonies as well as the pagan rites for the dead. "There can be neither Jew nor Greek, there can be neither slave nor freeman, there can be neither male nor female-for you are all one in Christ Jesus" (Galatians 3:28).

The Christian community of Korea as the servant community of the Spirit has the dual tasks of cultural ministry. One is the ministry of listening to the *han* cry of the dead in solidarity with Jesus who descended into hell. The other is the ministry of proclaiming the kingdom of God in obedience to Jesus who will come to judge the living and the dead. First and foremost, the Christian community of the Eucharist is the servant community led by the Spirit of the crucified, dead, buried, and risen Jesus. Up until the Reformation, "descended into hell" was confessed in between "dead and buried" and "on the third day rose from the dead." The clause means that Jesus enters in unbroken solidarity with those who have already died.[17] Jesus' descent into hell completes God's abandonment of Jesus expressed in the final words from the cross in the Gospel of Mark: "My God, my God, why has thou forsaken me?" (Mark 15:34). Jesus' unbroken solidarity with the dead, as revealed in his descent into hell, determines the character of the Christian community of faith as the servant community of the Spirit. The Spirit of Jesus, who descended into hell, passionately persuades the Christian community of faith to descend into the realm of the dead. The gesture of descending is that of a servant. Ministry as the function of the servant community of the Spirit is the ministry of listening. It is listening to the groans of the Spirit in the *han* cry of an Aunt Suni. Thus the ministry of the Spirit precedes the ministry of the Word. Here it means the ministry of holding one's tongue. What is required in the momentum of this ministry is not to convert an Aunt Suni to Christianity but to be completely open to the therapeutic and salvific presence and work of the Spirit by letting go of a Christian superiority complex and clerical arrogance and taking the form of servant. What is required of the members of the servant community is to give up the proud throne of the judge and to go down below with the lowly and the needy. "Mind not high things, but condescend to men of low estate" (Romans 12:16). The first service that the community of the Spirit owes to an Aunt Suni consists of listening to her. "Just as love to God begins with listening to His Word, so the beginning of love for the brethren is learning to listen to them" (Bonhoeffer).[18] Then how can we listen with the ears of God so that we may speak the Word of God?

The ministry of listening is not so much listening to the voices of the *han*-ridden spirits, which make one's hair stand on end, but listening to the stories of the *han*-ridden persons which are transmitted in the communities of memorial rite regardless of their religious background. The Christian community of the Eucharist should incorporate the intergenerational fellowship between the living and the dead into the *koinonia* of the saints which is guided by the Spirit. When the stories of dead ancestors are shared by living descendants, the Spirit of the crucified, dead, buried, and risen Jesus becomes the Mediator for the ministry of listening to, as well as speaking, the stories. The servant community of the Spirit which is obsessed with preaching the Word of God tends to consider the ministry of holding the tongue and listening a pre-stage for the ministry of proclamation, or a strategic retreat that allows for more speech in a later stage. To the contrary, the genuine ministry of holding the tongue and listening helps a sufferer like Aunt Suni speak up and cry out until her *han* cry turns into the groans of the Spirit. Unable to listen to such a *han* cry or to be patient and keep from speaking (Job 4:2), the "miserable comforters" (Job 16:2) usually criticize, in the name of the omnipotent God, the sufferer who is vexed with God and curses himself. What a sufferer like Aunt Suni desperately needs is someone to listen to her *han* cry.

Oh, that my words were recorded, that they were written on a scroll,
that they were inscribed with an iron tool on lead, or engraved in rock fever! . . .

Listen carefully to my words;
let this be the consolation you give me (Job 19:23-24, 21:2).

Why are the groans of the Spirit hidden deep inside the *han* cry of a sufferer? While going down to *Sheol*, unable to keep silent in the anguish of his spirit and in the bitterness of his soul, Job cries out "I despise my life; I would not live forever. Let me alone; my days have no meaning" (Job 7:16). Then how could this *han*-ridden person be assured of his future vindication by the Redeemer?:

> I know that my Redeemer lives, and that in the end he will stand upon the earth (Job 19:25).

The expectation of an eschatological salvation is not possible unless one is inspired by the Spirit of the Redeemer who went down to *Sheol* with him. Only when the servant community of the Spirit listens to the groans of the Spirit deep inside the *han* cry of a sufferer can it be engaged in the ministry of proclaiming the eternal Gospel of Jesus who descended into hell, yet will come again to judge the living and the dead. No community of faith will be exempted from the Last Judgment.

Listening to the story of Aunt Suni, we can and should recognize that her death was not merely the suicide of a neurotic but also a murder by the demonic forces of the tragic era of national division. She died while she was crawling over the hill of Arirang. Is there no hope left for the Aunt Sunis? How can the servant community of the Spirit minister to an Aunt Suni? How can the servant community dare to proclaim the Gospel of Jesus which turns her wailing into dancing? All these questions are derived from the incompleteness of her life which lacks restitution in history. Of course, it is important to organize a Korean version of 'the committee of truth and reconciliation like South Africa.' The eschatological vindication of her death, however, solely depends on Jesus' judgment of the living and the dead. For the time being she will have to be in the realm of the dead into which the Spirit of Jesus descended to preach the Gospel (1 Peter 3: 18-20). Therefore, the ministry of proclamation for an Aunt Suni may not go beyond the eschatological reminder of her healing and salvation.

> I praise you to the heights, Lord, for you will raise me up, you will not let my foes make merry over me. Lord, my God, I cried to you for help and you will heal me. Lord, you will lift me out of *Sheol,* from among those who will sink into oblivion you will give me life, (Psalm 30: 1-3 in the future tense).

"I believe in Jesus Christ,. . . ., was crucified, dead and buried, descended into hell,. . . ., He will come to judge the living and the dead." Let the Church say "Amen!"

1) Cf. Yun Sung-bum, *Korean Theology* (Sunmyungmunwhasa, 1972); Rhyu Dong-sik, *Road to Pungryu Theology* (Jeonmangsa, 1988); Park Pong-bae, *Christian Ethic and Korean Culture* (Sungkwangmunwhasa, 1983); Pyun Sun-whan, *Interreligious Dialogue and Asian Theology* (Korea Institute of Theology, 1996); Kim Kwang-sik, *Indigenization and Hermeneutics* (Korea Christian Publishing House, 1987); Hong Jung-su, *God the Weaver* (Chomyungmunwhasa, 1991); Lee Jung-bae, *Indigenization and Culture of Life* (Chongro Books, 1991).

2) Paul Tillich, *Systematic Theology*, vol. III (The University of Chicago Press, 1976), 248.

3) Cf. George A. Lindbeck, *The Nature of Doctrine* (The Westminster Press, 1984).

4) As the supreme deity *Hanunim* figured in the *Tangun* myth who is the grand son of *Hanunim*. *Tangun,* the first king of ancient Korea, was born between *Whanung* an illegitimate son of *Hanunim* and the Bear Woman. This myth is contained in the *Sanguk Yusa* (Remains of the Three Kingdoms) compiled by a Buddhist monk, Iron (1206-1289).

5) Hyun Ki-young, *Aunt Suni* (Changjakkwabipyungsa, 1979), 48-50.

6) Cf. Clifford Geertz, *The Interpretation of Cultures* (Basic Books, Inc., 19763).

7) C. S. Song, *Jesus in the Power of the Spirit* (Fortress Press, 1994), 158.

8) *Ibid.*

9) Kim Deuk-joong, *The Miracle Stories in the Gospels* (Concordia Press, 1996), 62.

10) Cf. Ahn Byung-mu, *Jesus of Galilee* (Korea Institute of Theology, 1993), 158-159.

11) Kim Seong-nae, *Chronicle of Violence, Ritual of Mourning: Cheju Shamanism in Korea* (The University of Michigan, 1989), 4.

12) Cf. Hyun Yong-joon, *A Study of Cheju Shamanism* (Chipmundang, 1986), 33.

13) Cf. Henry N. Smith, "Ancestor Practices in Contemporary Hong Kong: Religious Ritual or Social Custom?," *Asian Journal of Theology,* 3: 1 (1989): 31-45.

14) Cf. Ogasawara Masaru, "The Family and the Last Things: Family Ties and Christian Faith in the Resurrection of the Body As Seen against the Background of 'Ancestor Worship'," *The Japan Mission Journal,* 47 (1993): 18-31.

15) Cf. Johann Baptist Metz, *Faith in History and Society* (The Seabury Press, 1980).

16) Cf. Chung Hyun-kyung, "Welcome the spirit; hear her cries", *Christianity and Crisis,* vol. 51, No. 5 (1991): 220-227.

17) Cf. Theodore W. Jennings, Jr., *Loyalty to God* (Abingdon Press, 1992), 123-128.

18) Dietrich Bonhoeffer, *Life Together* (Harper & Row, 1954), 97.

CHAPTER 5

Theology of the Spirit and Political Theology

1. Orthodoxy, Orthopraxy, Orthopathy

THE HOLY SPIRIT movement of Korean church has been formed through three distinctive stages of development. The first stage of the formation of the Korean church began with the Bible-centered Great Revival in 1907. The second stage of the renewal of the Korean church was launched by the Rev. Lee Yong-do's prayer-centered reform movement in the 1930s. The third stage of the growth of the Korean church started as organization-centered pentecostalism in the 1960s. The gut feeling of Korean Christians, which grew out of the Holy Spirit movement, cannot and should not be defined either by mere orthodoxy or by orthopraxy. By the middle of the 1930s, the orthodoxy of the Korean Church developed into fundamentalism by means of which church authorities attacked the liberal theologians. However, it was neither orthodoxy nor liberalism that grasped the heart of the Korean Christian *minjung* at that time. It was rather the spiritual experience brought up by the Rev. Lee Yong-do's revivalism. Lee Yong-do's straightforward challenge against church authorities and his electrifying stimulation of religious passion long suppressed by the institution and the dogma of the church bore the fruits of a nationwide renewal of faith. *Minjung* theology as Korean political theology has been critical of the depoliticized escapism of revivalism in the 1930s. But it should be noted that the depoliticization of the Korean church had already begun after the March first independence movement in 1919 and it coincided with the emergence of socialism in the 1920s.

In the process of struggling against fundamentalist orthodox theology, which provides the backbone for the church authorities, *minjung* theologians lost sight of the evangelical gut feeling of the Korean church which grew out of the Holy Spirit movement. Of course, it is not right to claim

61

that *minjung* theology emphasizes orthopraxy at the cost of orthopathy (right feeling, right experience).[1] One of the unique characteristics of *minjung* theology among Third World theologies lies in the fact that the *han* experience of *minjung* is taken as the starting point for doing theology. The problem with *minjung* theology, however, comes from the question of how fitting is the *minjung* theological interpretation of *han* in the context of the evangelical gut feeling of the Korean church. *Han* refers to the feeling and experience of unjustifiable suffering. Since *han* is the feeling of the weak, who are exposed to oppression and suffering, *han* belongs to the gut feeling of lower-class people in society and to the Shamanistic tradition in religion. It is impossible to ignore the close ties of the history of the Holy Spirit movement with the Shamanistic *minjung* experience of *han*. Nevertheless, the Holy Spirit movement cannot be explained away by a mere Shamanistic phenomenon. The theological emphasis in the history of the early Korean church is on the repentance of sin and it is in tune with the prophetic, apostolic tradition of biblical Christianity. The lack of a hermeneutic of sin in *minjung* theology unnecessarily radicalized *minjung* theology so that it lost its Christian identity as well as its popular appeal.

The Holy Spirit movement of the Korean church has one thing in common with orthodoxy, namely, the *sola fide* tradition of the Reformation. *Minjung* theology tends to reduce the free grace of God through Christ into cheap grace, and faith in the merit of the blood of Jesus into magic. The focus of the second stage of the Holy Spirit movement was not the repentance of unbelievers but the repentance of believers. It reminds us of the Methodist movement in eighteenth century England. The Methodist movement was the repentance movement of nominal Christians whose renewal brought sociohistorical sanctification in England. The essence of the repentance movement is not a new message but a new presentation of the old message. When one challenges the dogmatic tradition of the established church, the appeal to the language and experience of the tradition is more effective than the total rejection of it. In this regard, the sectarian character of *minjung* theology hinders it from renewing the Korean church from within. Since the 1960s the *minjung* in the Korean church has been indulged with depoliticized pentecostalism while *the minjung* theologians have paid attention to the life and culture of the *minjung* outside of the Korean church. *Minjung* theology as an avant garde theology, which could not successfully inherit the progressive character of early Korean Christianity, ironically contributed to the depoliticization of the present Holy Spirit movement. The depoliticization of the Holy Spirit movement of the Korean church coincides with the 'ideologization' of *minjung* theology. For the last thirty years the Korean church was divided into the fundamentalist movement defending orthodoxy, the progressive movement of *minjung* theology seeking orthopraxy, and the pentecostal and church growth movement claiming the monopoly of orthopathy.

As the form of the Holy Spirit movement of the Korean church has changed every thirty years, we have to ask what form would be appropriate for the next generation in the twenty-first century. It should be sought in a form of orthopathy that combines orthodoxy and orthopraxy. One of the considerable changes which *minjung* theology is undergoing in the 1990s is that some of the *minjung* theologians have become open to a dialogue with orthodoxy. The external condition of this change is a result of the breakdown of cold war ideology which has imprisoned Christian faith in an era of national division on the one hand, and the growth of civil society which put an end to the military authoritarian regime on the other hand. Therefore, the orthodox conservative wing of the Korean church cannot insist on anticommunism any more, and the progressive *minjung* wing of the Korean church has to develop its flexibility in order to embrace the civic movements of conscientious middle-class people, *jungmin* in Korean. *Jungmin* is the group of people among the middle class who have *minjung* identity.[2] Since the end of the 1980s, *jungmin* has been active in various civil movements for economic justice, national reunification, environment, education, human rights, and culture. The maturation of civil society in the 1990s prepared a favorable environment for the Assembly of God in Korea, the most prominent pentecostal denomination to enter the National Council of Churches in Korea, which has represented the progressive movement of the Korean church. The leading force in the third stage of the Holy Spirit movement has become open to orthopraxy. Through opening itself to orthopraxy, the religious experience of depoliticized pentecostalism can become orthopathy. The theological task of the fourth stage of the Holy Spirit movement is how to combine orthodoxy and orthopraxy in terms of orthopathy.

The more biblical expression for orthopathy is orthosplanchna which refers to the compassionate feeling coming out of the guts. *Splanchni-zomai,* the verb form of *splanchna,* is used when Jesus had compassion on a large crowd in a remote place (Mark 6:34). It means the kind of compassion welling out of the depth of one's being. It is the gut reaction of a co-sufferer as if one has splitting intestines. Orthopathy as orthos-planchna is sympathy with the gut feeling of the suffering *minjung.* It is entering the feeling of the other so that one suffers with the other. This kind of compassion is not possible unless the Spirit of God is present in one's heart. Orthopathy is the spiritual sense which the Spirit of God creates in our spirits. Orthopathy is not a subjective feeling but a participation in *han* or the gut feeling of the other through the spiritual sense, namely, the heart of Jesus. Orthopathy as the recovery of the heart of Jesus is the middle ground between orthodoxy and orthopraxy.

Theodore Runyon describes the four characteristics of orthopathy in terms of "non-subjectivistic," "transformational," "social," and "teleological."[3] Appropriating the theory of communicative action, we may claim that orthodoxy lacking orthopathy becomes a theological form of systematically distorted communication.[4] The three conditions of ideal speech are the sincerity of the subjective world, the truthfulness of the objective world, and the legitimacy of the social world. These three conditions are related to orthopathy, orthodoxy, and orthopraxy respectively. The non-subjectivistic and social character of orthopathy means that the sincere orthopathy of the subjective world is combined with the truthful orthodoxy of the objective world. The transformational and theological character of orthopathy means that sincere orthopathy is combined with the legitimate orthopraxy of the social world. But orthodoxy without orthopathy is dogmatism and orthopraxy without orthopathy is ideocracy.

2. You Kill Jesus and Divide Up His Clothes, Modern Church!

The second stage of the Holy Spirit movement of the Korean church started in the spiritual crisis of the 1920s. Since the March 1st Movement in 1919, the Korean church, imprisoned by its institutionalization and dogmatization, had lost its spiritual power. Socialists and progressive intellectuals outside of the Korean church criticized the impotence of church to transform the colonial reality. In this pessimistic atmosphere Rev. Lee Yong-do (1901-1933) led the renewal movement of the Korean church. Before he entered the Methodist theological seminary in Seoul, he was an ardent nationalist who was imprisoned for three years after 1919. This is significant because his revivalism has been regarded as an escapist popular mysticism. Most of his critics who have the perspective of *minjung* theology consider Lee's movement to be as reactionary as the fundamentalist church authorities in the 1920s and 1930s. Instead, they take sides with the anti-ecclesiastical youth, intellectuals, laborers, and peasants who became socialists or communists. One cannot discern the genuinely progressive nature of Lee's Jesus movement, which grew out of orthopathy, as long as one is caught up in the dilemma of choosing between the orthodoxy of church authorities and the orthopraxy of anti-ecclesiastical groups. The main constituency of Lee's Jesus movement was the *minjung* of the Korean church in the 1930s. His movement can be properly understood not by the dialetic of theocentric orthodoxy and anthropocentric orthopraxy but by Spirit-centered orthopathy based on historical and cosmic divine-human participation. His contemporary social Gospel movement among Christian intellectuals could not persuade the *minjung* of the Korean church in opposition to orthodoxy. If one takes this fact into consideration, Lee's Jesus movement must have been a more threatening reform movement inside the institutionalized churches. Lee Yong-do did sympathize with the gut feeling of the Christian *minjung* and they were liberated from the western Caucasian image of Jesus with blue eyes and blonde hair which was introduced by the missionaries. In the history of the Korean church it was Lee Yong-do who drew and lived the Korean image of Jesus. He himself was an image of Jesus through whom the humble God was revealed. According to Lee, the humble God found his dwelling place in the poor and impoverished land of Asia since he could not stay in the Western world any more.

The political theological significance of Lee's Jesus movement lies in its challenge to the dominant structure of the Korean church in the 1930s. The socialists' and progressive Christian youths' anti-ecclesiastical critique of the ahistorical Korean church, which ignored the tragic reality of the colonialized nation, should not be blindly applied to Lee's Jesus movement. Lee's movement has the character of the *minjung* movement because it took part in the suffering *minjung* of the Korean church and criticized the hypocrisy of church authorities. Lee's Jesus movement as *minjung* movement has two sides. First of all, Lee distinguishes the true Jesus from the false Jesus and critically applies the distinction to the contemporary reality of the Korean church.

> Modern Christian demands false Jesus and modern minister preaches about false Jesus. If true Jesus comes, he cannot but be killed. Jesus whom they demand is Jesus of flesh, Jesus of glory, Jesus of riches, Jesus of honor. Jesus' own Jesus is Jesus of the Spirit, Jesus of lowliness, Jesus of poverty, Jesus of humility.[5]

The true Jesus for Lee Yong-do is the "servant of no word, humility, prayer, and obedience." Though he was a fluent revivalist who spoke like a machine gun, he nicknamed himself as Simeon (*si-mu-uhn* in Korean, which literally means person of no word) in the Gospel of Luke who had waited for the Messiah throughout his long life (Luke 2:25-35). Lee Yong-do experienced the power of the wordless Word on the cross. Lee once preached when his voice was completely gone. "Look, the wordless

Jesus! But listen to his wordless great sermon!" From the beginning of his revival in 1925 he could not help but pour out his tears when he tried to console the *han*-ridden people with the Word of God. He often went up to the pulpit only to pray passionately without preaching because he believed that true words are born by encountering God in silence. Lee Yong-do received the Word of God in the depth of the east Asian spirituality of nothingness or *sunyata,* where he could listen to the great preaching of the worldless Jesus.

What is the content of the worldless Jesus' sermon? It is first and foremost the humility that makes the self empty or nothing. Lee cried out "Jesus was originally rich, glorious, honorable, strong, and comfortable, but for us he became poor, shameful, downtrodden, weak, and uncomfortable." It is Jesus' *kenosis* (self-emptying), making himself nothing or *sunyata.* The self-emptying Jesus asks us to become nothing for Jesus as Jesus became nothing for us. Lee prayed, "Oh, Lord! I am nothing or *sunyata.* Let the Holy Spirit move over me in order to fulfill your vision and plan." Even when he was lying on his death bed, he put his hand over the head of a Bible woman to pray tearfully, "How many are those ladies dropping tears to seek their private blessing, and how numerous are those women not only destroying themselves but also murdering others! Oh, Lord! Thou have made her follow Jesus who killed his own body to save others. Please let her die beautifully on your way." Lee's self-emptying is not static self-negation but the *passio activa* of Jesus, which appears as prophetic indictment of injustice and priestly identification with sufferers. Lee pointed out the sins of his contemporary church leaders, missionaries, lay Christians, rich people, righteous ones, and white people who were fond of the false Jesus, and he asked them to repent. But he embraced the pains of beggars, prostitutes, clowns, the sick, sinners, blacks, and women, and he tried to learn from them and to listen to the voice of the Lord dwelling in them. His critique of the established churches was so severe that those church leaders who felt threatened by it attempted to check and condemn him. Because Lee believed that what the contemporary church needed most was not the pioneers of dogma or of organizations but those of the repentance movement, he strongly demanded the repentance of Korean Christians who "have the dry bones of dogma and creed in their heads like an old tree and whose spirits have lost their life to become petrified." Here again we find that Lee's critique of orthodoxy was based on orthopathy, namely, the heart of Christ.

> Evil church longed for and boasted about dogma and creed at her pulpit, but she lost the heart of Christ! Faith means . . . that the heart of Christ

becomes my heart, and the Spirit of Christ becomes my spirit so that I am willing to die for the love of God and human being. How an arrogant church dare to claim she loves them?[6]

Orthodoxy without the orthopathy of the Korean church in the 1920s was impotent. It was like the hypocrisy of the Pharisees in Jesus' times who were not able to communicate with *minjung (ochlos)* suffering under Roman imperialism. The authorities of the Korean church were only concerned about an escapist evangelism controlled by fundamentalist orthodoxy. Especially since the failure of the March 1st Movement, not Christianity but socialism grasped the hearts of progressive youth as well as intellectuals. The Korean socialists of the 1920s were like Zealots in Jesus' time. They condemned the Korean church which became "the limbs of imperialism and the weapons securing capitalist state." Lee Yong-do's Jesus movement as the orthopathic movement of renewing the heart of Christ in the Korean church can be best understood in the theological and political dilemma between ecclesiastical orthodoxy and socialist orthopraxy.

The majority of the Korean *minjung* in the 1920s were farmers who constituted eighty percent of the Korean population. After the March 1st Independence Movement, the Japanese colonial regime disguised its imperialistic ambition with so-called 'cultural politics'. Cultural politics provided window dressing but did not change the substance of its colonial policy at all. Misled nationalists appeared who insisted a gradual reform was possible. Contrary to their pro-Japanese expectation, the Japanese imperialistic control of the Korean economy became worse in the 1920s. Mainland Japan failed in her domestic economic policy around the year 1918. Japanese capitalists allied with Japanese semi-feudal landlords. The contradictions of Japanese semi-feudalistic-authoritarian capitalism became clear in the imbalance between fast industrial growth and the shortage of food caused by both the decrease of agricultural production under semi-feudal landlordship and the rapid increase of the population of major industrial cities in Japan. The Japanese capitalist government did not attempt to solve the socioeconomic crisis with land reform for productive agriculture and democratization for the rights of laborers. Instead, Japanese capitalists turned themselves into aggressive imperialists to exploit the agricultural production of their colonies. For instance, 56.8% of agricultural production in Korea was 'exported' (forcefully delivered) to Japan in 1931. In turn Korean farmers became bankrupt because they could not pay the debts which were forced on them in the name of increasing agricultural production. Korean farmers who lost their land either became the *lumpen* proletariat of the Japanese colonial capitalist machine or emigrated to Manchuria and Japan only to suffer as low-wage foreign laborers.

Despite its stark opposition to the impotent orthodoxy of the Korean church, the orthopraxy of Korean socialists should not be played down by any serious Korean theologian. Of course, there were some uncompromising Christian nationalists who cooperated with socialists in their common struggle against Japanese imperialism. Shinkanhoe, which represented the nationalist-socialist united front, was organized in 1927, but it was unfortunately dissolved in 1931, the peak year of Lee's Jesus movement and the fateful year of the Korean history of ideological division. The dissolution of Shinkanhoe was very tragic for the Korean nation and the Korean *minjung*. It was the creative, united leadership of Shinkanhoe that guided tenant disputes and labour disputes as well as student demonstrations, which reached their peak between the last half of the 1920s and the first half of the 1930s. During this period, it was not the Korean church but Shinkanhoe that was persecuted by Japanese police. The strengthening of ecclesiastical authoritarianism in the 1920s and 1930s was connected to the subtle conspiracy of cultural politics. The Japanese government-general changed the license system of establishing a new church into the report system. Pro-Japanese missionaries and church leaders welcomed this change and were completely co-opted by Japanese cultural politics. Despite Japanese protection of the interests of church authorities and the church leaders' enthusiastic efforts for church growth, church growth visibly slowed while the number of missionaries and paid ministers increased.

There were both external and internal causes of the tragic dissolution of Shinkanhoe. Japanese imperialism severely persecuted it because it had awakened the political consciousness of the Korean *minjung* struggling against Japanese colonial rule. The internal cause came not only from Christian nationalists' hegemonism but also from extreme leftists' adventurism. Nevertheless, the great leaders of Shinkanhoe, such as Lee Sang-jae and Hong Myung-hi, proposed the ideological telos of a national movement for the anti-imperialistic, anti-feudalistic, and anti-capitalistic liberation of the Korean *minjung*. This ideological front of three *min* (*minjok* or nationalism, *minjung* liberation, *minju* or democracy) was the guiding principle of the Shinkanhoe movement in the 1920s, the left-right solidarity movement for a unified nation around the year 1945, and the radical movement of democratization and national reunification in the 1980s. It must be noted that the ideal of three *min* could not captivate the heart of the Korean *minjung*, not only

68

because of the extremely severe police surveillance of socialists by the Japanese government-general, but also because of the fundamental religiousness of the Korean *minjung*, which resisted the Korean socialists' atheistic interpretation of human existence. The orthopraxy of Shinkanhoe and of other progressive movements, based on the ideology of three *min*, became empty because it lost touch with the gut feeling of the Korean *minjung*. Especially Korean communists' dogmatic orthopraxy, which excluded all non-proletarian nationalism and resulted in a stubborn and unproductive ideocracy.

Unlike Lee Yong-do's passionate criticism of the Korean church, his attitude toward *minjung* was humility itself. Calling himself "an eternally least, stupidest, and least student," he declared that "all children, beggars, prostitutes, insects, animals, trees, and grasses are my teacher." Since he believed that the Spirit of the Lord was present among all the sick, the poor, and the sinners, Lee could appeal to the *minjung* of the Korean church with the truth of Jesus' Passion in the very midst of the tragic reality of the Korean nation.

> We are a weak nation and a slave in the world, bearing our cross. Like a dumb you say no word when you are stricken and afflicted on behalf of us. We silently adore you. The pagan ruler puts a crown of thorns around our head and we are forced by him to lie down on the socially lowest bed of nails. . . .Oh, loving teacher! Come down into our heart. Teach us the *Tao* of servanthood even for lepers and underdogs, your love enduring all hardship and embracing the whole world.[7]

Lee Yong-do's interpretation of the cross is so unique that it can provide an orthopathic alternative to the dilemma of choosing between the orthodox interpretation of the cross in pentecostalism and the orthopraxic interpretaion of the cross in *minjung* theology in the third stage of the Holy Spirit movement of the Korean church. What he asked of the suffering *minjung* was to follow the suffering Jesus, to believe and to follow the Lord of the Passion so that the grace of atonement and the calling of discipleship are united. Some pentecostal enthusiasts believe that Jesus' once-and-for-all sacrifice on the cross is enough for pardoning sin. They reject the presence of Jesus' cross in every age when Christians confess the crucified Jesus as their Lord and fulfill their discipleship in following Jesus. For instance, the Pure Gospel Church, whose pastor is Cho Yong-gi, reduces the meaning of the hymn about Christian discipleship into an antinomian theory of atonement. "Call'd of God, we honor the call," says one of the popular Korean hymns written by Lee Ho-uhn who was affected by Lee Yong-do in his youth. The third stanza of the hymn goes as follows:

> Honor, glory, power and praise/Lord to you, you only are due!
> Shame and scorn and cross/Grant us grace to carry them too,
> Without name or fame, but oh Lord,/Joy and thanks to serve before you
> Without name or fame, but oh Lord,/Joy and thanks to serve before you!

The pentecostalists changed the second line of the above hymn into "Shame and scorn and cross / the Lord already carried them." This change reminds us of the Corinthian enthusiasts who cursed the crucified Jesus and got excited in the Spirit of the exalted Christ (1 Corinthians 12:3). The above hymn is inspired by Lee Yong-do's unique interpretation of the cross which typically represents the paradigm of Korean theology of the Spirit, i.e., the cosmic, historical divine-human participation. In the history of the church Lee distinguishes the first age of the church represented by Peter, the second age of monasticism represented by James, the third age of faith (Reformation priod) represented by Paul, and the fourth age of love (the present time) represented by John. Lee's description of the age of love is in line with John Wesley's theology of evangelical synergism. The essence of the age of love lies in the maturation of "faith working in love" (Galatians 5:6). It does not eliminate the Reformation message, justification by grace through faith. Presupposing faith in the cross of atoning grace, it asks for Christian perfection in the sense that we have the heart of Christ and follow the Lord in his footsteps.

Pointing out the defect of false faith without love, Lee lamented, "By the courage and guts out of faith one can fight against sin and reproach a sinner; but alas!, one cannot have mercy on a sinner." True faith, according to Lee, comes out of "the death of oneself for the love of God and human being which is possible when the heart of Christ becomes my heart and the Spirit of Christ becomes my spirit." Lee's description of true faith refers to an orthopathic standpoint combining the orthodoxy of faith in the merit of Christ with the orthopraxy of love dying for the body of Christ. It should not be confused with the liberal interpretation of the moral teaching of Jesus which has nothing to do with faith in the atonement by Christ. Despite its contribution to the correction of orthodoxy by means of orthopraxy, *minjung* theology still keeps the liberal bias in the interpretation of the cross. A prominent *minjung* theologian rejected the orthodox dogma that "Jesus of Nazareth expiated for and on behalf of my sin." Instead, he claimed that "I reenact Jesus and Jesus event is now occurring again." To identify Jesus even in *the minjung* event without presupposing Jesus' atonement will result in the absolutization of the *minjung* as well as the self-righteousness of the *minjung* movement because *minjung* theologians only see the *han* of the *minjung* and won't see the sin of the *minjung*.

Lee's identification of the suffering *minjung* as well as Lee himself with the suffering Jesus is not a matter of unitive mysticism but of sacramental divine-human participation.

> You kill Jesus and divide up his clothes, modern church! You throw away Jesus' blood and flesh and take its form and ritual. And still you are proud of what you're doing, gangs of modern church! What has been your real intention to believe in Jesus?[8]

What did make Lee Yong-do see the crucified Jesus in the suffering *minjung*, and the ones who crucified Jesus in the gangs of the Korean church? It was none other than Jesus' compassionate heart touched by the *ochlos* like sheep without a shepherd. Jesus' heart became connected with the gut feeling of the *minjung* which brought about the miracle of feeding them in wilderness. As the hungry and wandering *minjung* in Jesus' times were oppressed and exploited by Roman imperialism and the religious status quo of the Jerusalem temple, the hungry and wandering *minjung* in Korea in the 1920s were not only exploited by Japanese imperialism but also deserted by the orthodox status quo of the Korean church. The spiritual meaning of Jesus' institution of the Eucharist is the "unity of meal and sacrifice" (Kim Ji-ha) because Jesus shared his own flesh and blood through sharing ordinary bread and wine. Contrary to this unity of meal and sacrifice, the Jewish religious leaders did not understand the *han* of the hungry *minjung* wandering in the wilderness and excluded them from their temple worship. The orthodox authorities of the Korean church also created the demonic gap separating meal and sacrifice. Those who "kill Jesus and divide up his clothes" and "throw away Jesus' blood and flesh and take its form and ritual" rejected the true Jesus who was present in the suffering *minjung* and received the false Jesus who was present in the idol worship of those taking away rice from the poor. Lee's Jesus movement challenged the idol worship of the false Jesus. Where is the true Jesus in the present Korean church? Is the true Jesus absent or is he imprisoned in the cement sculpture of the "gold-crowned Jesus" (Kim Ja-ha)? How long have the orthodox authorities of the Korean church been maids for the authoritarian state power idolizing anticommunism in the age of national division? Has not the true Jesus, who is the friend of a leper, a beggar, and

71

a prostitute, disappeared? Isn't it the false Jesus, protected by a priest, a company president, and a policeman, who is left?

3. Destroy This Temple!

Jesus speaks the same words, "Destroy this temple!" (John 2: 19), to the church which is proud of being the body of Christ yet has already lost the heart of Christ. The story of Jesus cleansing the temple in the Gospel of John appears in the beginning of Jesus" activity because its meaning is considered directly related to the very meaning of the life, death, and resurrection of Jesus. Jesus' words about destroying the temple were one of the fatal reasons for his death (Matthew 26:61-62). They directly challenged the religious and political status quo of the Jerusalem temple and the Jewish priests condemned Jesus' blasphemy, i.e., Jesus' self-styled messiahship (Matthew 22:64-65).

The story of Jesus cleansing the temple (John 2) is closely related to those stories that follow it, Jesus teaching Nicodemus (John 3) and Jesus meeting a Samaritan woman (John 4). The fact that even the early Christian community realized the meaning of Jesus' identification of the temple with his own body *(soma)* only after the Resurrection (John 2:21-22) makes us aware of how threatening Jesus' words "Destroy this temple" were to the Jewish authorities of Jerusalem temple. Through these consecutive stories the Johannine community clearly demonstrates how to destroy the old temple based on patriarchy and master-slave relationships as well as how to build the new temple of equality and mutual love. The story of Nicodemus and that of a Samaritan woman are contrasting but closely related texts. Nicodemus was a man of the Pharisees and a member of the Jewish ruling council, but an anonymous Samaritan woman was a poor, pagan prostitute. Nicodemus, who came to Jesus at night, heard Jesus' teaching but did not understand, while the Samaritan woman who met Jesus at noon received Jesus' teaching and became its living witness. The failure of Nicodemus represents the decaying system of the Jerusalem temple which eventually killed Jesus. And the success of the Samaritan woman represents the new community of equal partners in which the resurrected Spirit of Jesus was present.

If we once again listen to Jesus' words "Destroy this temple!" in the present situation of the Korean church, who is the representative of the old temple to be destroyed and who represents the new temple to be built? Yu Choon-ja, a Korean woman theologian who was the general secretary of the Korean Woman Theologians' Association for many years, identifies the old Korean comfort women abused in the Japanese prostitution army during World War II as Samaritan women in our times.[9] As a Samaritan woman was excluded from the religious community of the Jerusalem temple by the holiness code of Judaism, oppressed by patriarchal culture, and politically and economically alienated by Roman imperialism, the old Korean comfort women were exploited by the Japanese imperialistic war machine, discriminated against by the patriarchal culture of shame after they survived the war, and discarded by the Korean church. Thus, the old Korean comfort women have become the *minjung* of the *minjung* in Korea. As a Samaritan woman came to Jacob's well to draw water at noon, which was an unlikely time for an ordinary Jewish woman to come to the well, the old Korean comfort women have protested since 1990 against the Japanese government in front of the Japanese embassy in Seoul at noon every Wednesday, which is the comfortable lunch hour for ordinary old Korean women. Thanks to the old Korean comfort women's courageous action demanding an apology and compensation from the Japanese government for committing the crime of sex slavery during the war, a bill of Japanese sexual war crimes was adopted by the U. N. Commission on Human Rights. The old Korean comfort women have become the mothers of the world as well as of Korea so that they indict not only sexual violence and crime committed against the Korean, Chinese, and other foreign female labourers in Korea, but also sexual war crimes all over the world.

The Johannine community contrasted the story of Nicodemus with that of the Samaritan woman in order to distinguish the old temple to be destroyed from the new temple to be built. Nicodemus' failure to understand the truth of being born through water and the Spirit (John 3:4-5) was deeply connected with the rejection of Jesus by the system of the Jerusalem temple which resulted in its own downfall (John 3:18-19). The downfall of the Jerusalem temple system is the meaning of baptism in the sense that to be born through water and the Spirit presupposes the death of the old self and of the old community on the cross. Nicodemus in the present Korean context is the members as well as the leaders of what Lee Yong-do called the modern church which kills Jesus and divides up his clothes. Those Korean Christians who desert the true Jesus, i.e., Jesus of the poor, the downtrodden, and the humiliated, and welcome the false Jesus, i.e., Jesus of the rich, the powerful, and the privileged are Nicodemus and his friends. But "what is born of flesh is flesh; what is born of the Spirit is spirit." (John 3:6). The false Jesus is Jesus of the flesh and the true Jesus is Jesus of the Spirit.

73

Jesus was perplexed by Nicodemus' spiritual ignorance and rebuked what Nicodemus represented, namely, the Pharisees'' sins of hypocrisy and disbelief, and he warned them of divine condemnation. However, Jesus' attitude toward the Samaritan woman was incredibly merciful and generous. Jesus demanded that the orthodox Jew Nicodemus and the orthodox Korean church repent and bear the fruits of repentance. But Jesus, who shared the Samaritan woman's gut feeling of *han,* did not condemn her; instead, he persuaded her to confess her sin and guided her to surrender her own body to true worship in spirit and truth. The scheme of divine-human participation which undergirded the encounter between Jesus and a Samaritan woman disclosed a thoroughly Spirit-centered interaction. In their dialogue on several topics the three conditions of the ideal speech situation were fully satisfied. The sincerity of their subjective world, the truthfulness of their objective world, and the legitimacy of their social world were well demonstrated in their communicative praxis. Neither manipulation nor systematically distorted communication hindered their mutual interaction. In their discussion about water, Jesus did not one-sidedly provide her with "a spring of water, welling up for eternal life" (John 4: 15). Instead, being tired from his journey, Jesus first asked her, "Give me something to drink" (John 4:7). This radically manifested the humanity of Jesus and the presence and work of the Spirit in the depth of the Samaritan woman. Being crucified at around noon, Jesus said on the cross, "I am thirsty" (John 19: 28). Why did the Johannine community synchronize the hour of Jesus' desperate experience of thirst on the cross with the hour of his feeling thirsty at Jacob's well? At the very hour the Samaritan woman came to the well to draw water to avoid shame and scorn, Jesus on the cross experienced the utmost shame and scorn and bled and thirsted.

The Samaritan woman represents a new being for which the Johannine community strived, a new community as well as a new person. She represents the new temple built by being born through water and the Spirit. Her being was deeply rooted in the spring of water welling up for eternal life. Here the spring of living water indicates an orthopathic change at the gut level. Lee Yong-do claimed that such a radical change of being took place in Christian prayer. He called it 'exchange of life' in the sense that "we constantly find out iniquity in our life and come to Jesus in our prayer to change it with his life and righteousness." Unlike an arbitrary exchange rate for the currency of a poor nation in the capitalist money market, the exchange rate in such a divine-human encounter is full of grace and truth. The thirst of the Samaritan woman was exchanged for eternal life by the spring of living water. Her thirst, her life, and her being were led by the Spirit to a blessed intersubjectivity which interacted with Jesus' thirst, Jesus' life, and Jesus' being. The orthopathic change of a Samaritan woman brought about the creative combination of orthodoxy and orthopraxy. Through the orthopathic change her sincerity qua faith of her subjective world came into contact with the divine sincerity or faithfulness of Jesus. Only then did her witness of the Gospel become truthful and legitimate. Her being together with Jesus was the new temple, the new community of faith and love. Her witness to the people of Samaria, "Come, see a man who told me everything I ever did. Could this be the Christ?" (John 4:29), does not indicate any authoritarian, dogmatic gesture. The truthfulness of her witness comes from her being together with Jesus, an objective reference of her witness. This discloses the equal partnership the Johannine community sought. She dared to reveal her shame, which was shared by her partner Jesus' experience of shame on the cross, and witness to Jesus as the Christ. Yes, the legitimacy of evangelism in the social world can be earned only when the Samaritan woman is not only included but also considered an equal partner in the faith community.

The old Korean comfort women's protest at noon every Wednesday in front of the Japanese embassy is a political event because it reveals what is really shameful, namely, patriarchal culture and imperialism. It is also a theological event because the authentic meaning of the Crucifixion of Jesus is reincarnated in this historic place of shame and protest at the same hour. The God who comes to the old Korean comfort women at noon every Wednesday is not a God reigning with power and glory but the crucified and thirsty God crawling over the hill of Arirang. Today Jesus appears to those women, saying, "Give me something to drink." Orthopathic change in the Korean church is possible only when she becomes open to the spring of living water in the midst of those women. The truthfulness of her evangelism and the legitimacy of her social mission depend on the solidarity of the Korean church with those women who are together with Jesus.

---

1) Orthopathy is the term phrased by Theodore Runyon. Cf. his unpublished lecture on "J. D. Northey Lectures 1993: Wesleyan resources for ecumenical theology."

2) Cf. Han Sang-jin, "Survey on a centralizing model of social transformation: toward the *jungmin* line," *The Thought,* Summer, 1989.

3) Cf. T. Runyon, *op. cit.,* pp. 33-40.

4) Cf. Juergen Habermas, *The Theory of Communicative Action,* Vol. 2 (Beacon Press, 1987).

5) Jesus Church, ed., *The Writings of the Rev. Lee Yong Do: Si-mu-uhn* (Dasan Publishing House, 1993), p. 61.

6) Pyun Jong-ho, ed., *The Letters of Lee Yong-do* (Chosuk Publishing House, 1986), p. 67.

7) Pyun Jong-ho, ed., *The Journal of the Rev. Lee Yong-do* (Chosuk Publishing House, 1986), p. 67.

8) *Ibid.,* p. 941.

9) Cf. Yu Choon-ja, "A study of a Korean Samaritan woman," *Korean Feminist Theology,* December, 1996.

CHAPTER 6

Theology of the Spirit and Religious Pluralism

1. Faith of *Ilsaghakoh* (Faith Daring to Die Once) and Confucian Christianity

ELEBRATING THE CENTENNIAL anniversary of the Rev. Martyr Chu Ki-chul'sbirth.

Both Korean exclusivists who disdain religious pluralism and Korean pluralists who consider exclusivist religious ideology good-for-nothing have one thing in common. They fail to recognize the significant fact that the exclusive attitude of the Korean church toward other religions is the product of religious pluralism in Korea. Such exclusivism has been known as the child of a puritanical faith supported by conservative orthodox theology. But this does not explain why such a phenomenon has appeared in the Korean church which has not been merely a passive recipient of the Gospel brought by missionaries. As a matter of fact, the major religious-cultural ethos of the Korean church as an active participant in the Gospel has come from Confucianism. It was not an accident but the work of the Holy Spirit that many Korean Christians, whose form of faith consisted of both a conservative Christian worldview and the Confucian ethos, firmly insisted on the mutual incompatibility of the required Japanese emperor worship at the Shinto shrine and the Lordship of Jesus Christ. This led to a monumental history of martyrdom with tears and blood. The Rev. and martyr Chu Ki-chul's (1897-1944) faith of *ilsaghakoh* (daring to die once), which is the *locus classicus* of the prophetic protest of the Korean church over against worshiping at the Shinto shrine, most clearly manifests the Confucian ethos of 'great righteousness and chastity" melted and mixed by the Spirit with conservative orthodox faith daring to die in order to overcome the forced idolatry of Japanese imperialism.

I can never live a life to bow the knee to other gods except my Lord. I would rather die and die again to keep my chastity for my Lord than live a filthy life. . . . I have no choice but daring to die once. A pine tree cut down before it dies is vivid blue, a lily fallen down before it withers is fragrant. . . . May my body be a sacrifice on the Lord's altar before it withers away![1]

In Chu Ki-chul's last sermon, "Five Themes of My Prayer," Deutronomic theology of divine sovereignty and theology of the cross calling for participation in the suffering of Jesus Christ are fused in the Confucian ethos of righteousness and chastity. It was caused by the operation of the Holy Spirit which grasped the personal faith of Chu Ki-chul. The historical divine-human participation guided by the Sprit was evident in the mysterious and providential harmony of the Confucian ethos, Christian nationalism, and conservative orthodox faith in forming his personality and faith. Chu Ki-chul's greatness arose when the conflict between the Lordship of Christ and emperor worship happened to mirror the tensions between his restless, brilliant personality and his tragic environment under Japanese imperialism.

Chu Ki-chul was a descendent of the famous Chinese Confucian scholar Chu Hsi (1130-1200). There were 39 generations from Chu Hsi to Chu Ki-chul. Chu Hsi's grandson Chu Jam and his son Yeo-kyung and eight other literati emigrated from China to Korea in 1224. It is well known that Confucianism, especially neo-Confucianism completed by Chu Hsi, was most influential in Korea among the three northeastern countries. As Tu Weiming said, "Among all the dynasties, Chinese and foreign, the long-lived Chosun (Yi) in Korea (1392-1910) was undoubtedly the most thoroughly Confucianized."[2] Confucianism, although it originated in China, was one of many cultural factors and never took as strong a hold on the Chinese culture as it did on the Korean culture during the last dynasty. In Japan, where neo-Confucianism was primarily a concern of the ruling elite and the associated literati class, it never enjoyed orthodox status as it did in Korea. As J. H. Grayson properly claimed, "It is only in Korea that we find a society in which the predominant political, cultural, and social influences were and are Confucian."[3]

Chu Ki-chul was born in a small village, Woongchun, belonging to the southeast province of Korea, on November 25, 1897, three days after the national funeral ceremony of the last Korean queen murdered by the Japanese. Scores of Chu families who shared their proud last name had held a memorial service for Chu Hsi twice a year since the seventeenth century. However, Woongchun was a village of humiliation and a place of national *han*. Konishi, one of the generals of the Japanese invaders, built a wall and a house in Japanese style and stayed in Woongchun from 1595 to 1598. Many Korean scholars, craftsmen, and ceramists were taken by Konishi to Japan. Being proud of their ancestry yet hurt by the sixteenth century Japanese invasion, the indignation and protest of the Chu families against Japanese imperialism was peculiar. Chu Ki-chul went to Kaetong elementary school which was founded by his relative Chu Ki-hyo, an ardent member of the national religion, Eastern Learning. A history teacher at the school made his students, including Chu Ki-chul, aware of the national distinction between Koreans and Japanese when they made field trips to the age-old ruins of the Japanese invasion during the time of the new Japanese aggression. Chu Ki-chul was born just three hundred years after Konishi left Woongchun in 1598 to become a good shepherd of judgment and atonement for the Korean people, sacrificing himself for the sake of faith and conscience, and of patriotism and loyalty. Consequently, Min Kyung-bae asserts that "the greatest historical conflict fought and won by the truth and faith of martyr Chu Ki-chul resolved the three hundred year old *han* and brought to our 'white-clad folk' (Korean people) the sublime moral victory which became a milestone in the history of new Korea."[4]

The most significant clue to understanding the faith development of young Chu Ki-chul is shame. Shame is popular these days in the theology of pastoral care as well as in psychotherapy. According to the dominant view, influenced by psychoanalyst Sigmund Freud and cultural anthropologists Margaret Mead and Ruth Benedict, Western culture is guilt-driven while Eastern culture is shame-driven, and guilt is thought to be a more profound emotional state than shame. The guilt-driven culture produces an inner-directed person who internalizes the norms of society and feels remorse when he or she contravenes his or her conscience. But the shame-driven culture produces an outer-directed person with a less developed conscience who feels no remorse by breaking the rules. But is it really true that saving face is more Western? Such cultural prejudice is caused by the lack of a deeper understanding of shame. Freudian psychology and the associated theology of pastoral care, which consider the self basically narcissistic, is both a theological and an anthropological mistake.

A deeper understanding of shame began to emerge in the 1970s after the American defeat in Vietnam. American veterans of the war in Vietnam in particular and American people in general lost their sense of identity and experienced shame. Such an experience of shame included the exposure of their weakness, a glimpse of their own shadow, betrayal, and abandonment. "Of those Americans who fought, twice as many as were killed in action have since committed suicide, and one-third of the nation's three to five million homeless people are Vietnam veterans."[5] Many people are also seeing psychic, physical, or sexual abuse in their own childhood with new eyes, namely, in terms of the relationships between abuse, shame, and addiction. According to Erik Erikson's study of child psychology, shame emerges during the period when the child first becomes consciously aware of the evaluations of others--between eighteen and twenty-four months of age. Though shame as a kind of evaluative self-consciousness is painful, it provides a foundational element for conscience. Guilt, emerging between ages three and five, has to do with self-judgment and remorse about violating rules or about consciously injuring others. In other words, guilt is about something I have done or contemplated doing; shame is about something I am or am not. Proper shame serves as the guardian of the self in its relations to others and to God, but cycles of bypassed or unacknowledged personal or collective shame fuel the clan warfare and violence in Somalia and the bloody ethnic cleansing in Bosnia.[6]

The essential element in Chu Ki-chul's faith of *ilsaghakoh* is the Confucian ethos of righteousness qua chastity. According to Mencius, the clue for righteousness is *suohjishim* (the heart of shame and aversion). The experience of shame permeated Chu Ki-chul's existence and his national identity and affected his conversion to the Christian faith. In his sermon "The Second Coming of the Lord," based on 1 Peter 3, he talks about the eschatological judgment of the unfaithful Christians by alluding to the shame of a woman who loses her chastity.

> Suppose a woman whose husband went far to make money had an affair with another man, what a shame and what a pity when her husband would suddenly return home in great glory! So we the bride of the Lord should not lose the devoted heart for the Lord even in the most severe adversity and keep our chastity carefully so that we might receive the Lord without shame.[7]

"Contemplation on Suffering" is Chu Ki-chul's own autograph statement warning himself of the shame he would go through at the end of the world if he refused suffering and martyrdom.

> If I avoid "suffering for the sake of the Lord" now, how shall I face the Lord later? If I avoid "imprisonment for the sake of the Lord" now, how shall I answer to the Lord who will ask me later, "Where is the cup of suffering after you enjoyed your peaceful life in my name?" If I avoid "cross for the sake of the Lord" now, how shall I answer to the Lord who will ask me later, "Where is the cross of suffering the only inheritance I gave you?"[8]

The interpretation of shame in Western theology has centered around the story of the Fall in Genesis. Interpreting the passage that the eyes of Adam and Eve who disobeyed God were opened and they realized they were naked (Gen. 3:7), Bonhoeffer says, "Shame is man's uneffaceable recollection of his estrangement," and reminds man of "his disunion with God and with other men."[9] What is significant is that shame emerges when man's original relation with 'Thou' is broken. A proper understanding of shame presupposes a theological anthropology viewing man as a relational being. According to Barth, the human being is the covenant partner of God and he or she becomes human only when he or she is with other human beings. Barth criticizes liberal theology, which is based on the kind of humanism culminating in Nietzsche's superman without fellow humans. Barth, however, affirms that theological anthropology needs to listen carefully to those who describe humanity in a very similar way but from a very different angle, i.e., the pagan Confucius, the atheist L. Feuerbach, and the Jew M. Buber. According to these three, man is human because of the fact that he is with his fellowman gladly. Barth claims that even "the sinner is capable of humanity in the sense of that freedom of the heart for others."[10] In the doctrine of reconciliation, Barth calls the wisdom we encounter in the non-Christian sphere "parables of the Kingdom." In fact, "the speech of Jesus Christ attested by the ministry of the Christian community" is carried out by "human words which attest the one Word of God and can thus be regarded as 'parables of the Kingdom.'"[11] Such wisdom as parables of the kingdom will guide the progress of the Church, "not to break continuity with the insights of preceding fathers and brethren, but in obedience to the one Lord of the Church and in the discipleship of the prophets and apostles to take it up and continue it with new responsibility on the basis of better instruction."[12] Barth perceives the *Geist* of Jesus who told the parables of the kingdom which came from non-religious, secular, and ordinary experiences. The above quoted Chu Ki-chul's discourse on shame at the end of the world not only concurs with the spirit of Jesus' parables but also suggests an eschatological interpretation of shame.

When he talks about shame, Chu Ki-chul's allusion to a woman who loses her chastity does not simply reflect the Confucian ethos. The deeper structure of his parabolic imagination is rooted in Jesus' parables of the kingdom such as the parable of ten virgins (Matthew 25:1-13), the parable of the wedding clothes (Matthew 22: 11-14), and the parable of the faithful and unfaithful servants (Matthew 24:45-51, Luke 12:42-46). Chu Ki-chul's own autograph statement, "Contemplation on Suffering," might not have been written if he had not meditated on the parable of the last

Judgment (Matthew 25:31-46). He took the parabolic image of separating the sheep from the goats into his heart so seriously and thoroughly that he would rather avoid shame and humiliation when facing the Lord in his judgment seat than avoid the present suffering, imprisonment, and cross. It should not be forgotten that Chu Ki-chul's understanding of the parable was not only related to the Confucian ethos but also was born in his concrete desperate situation of martyrdom. He nicknamed himself *soyang* (Jesus' sheep). The most important metaphor in his thought is *I* (righteousness) whose Chinese character consists of *yang* (sheep) and *a'* (self). Calling himself Jesus' sheep demonstrates his determination to go through all suffering, imprisonment, and cross now in order to overcome eschatological shame later. What is significant here is that Chu Ki-chul's parable of a unchaste woman and his autograph "Contemplation on Suffering" are very fitting ways of interpreting the parabolic spirit of Jesus, namely, Jesus' original message of the kingdom, for the Korean people who are permeated with the Confucian ethos. Chu Ki-chul warned Korean Christians, who lost their nation and felt shame and humiliation, of the danger of idolatry which would cause the eschatological shame that would lose the kingdom of God. His manner of preaching was too solemn and resolute for words.

No one can properly understand the quintessence of the song of Arirang which carries the *han* of the Korean *minjung* unless one notices the shame of the one who is abandoned by one's lover. This *stimmung* (moods) of Arirang is well manifested in Chu Ki-chul's sermon, "One Hundred and Twenty Year Long Life of Moses." Chu Ki-chul describes the heart of Moses who had to leave his people after he killed an Egyptian who was persecuting Jews as the following.[13]

"Going, going, I'm going/Leaving my lover behind, I'm going.

Abandoning his beloved compatriots, Moses wept every ten miles, cried every hundred miles. Crossing over to Midian, lo!, it was a lonesome wilderness. What a shame a hero was adopted by Jethro as husband for an heiress!"

The song of *Arirang*, the song of *han* and shame, was transformed into the song of Exodus, the song of calling and rapture, by Chu Ki-chul who obeyed the commandment of God to liberate Korean Christians from the idolatry of Japanese imperialism.

"I am sending you to Pharaoh to lead my people the Israelites out of Egypt,". . . . It was the greatest commandment of God, and Moses obeyed it. "Since God calls me . . . and the fate of our nation hangs by a thread, I will go though I may die. I will go with the Lord."

What was the fate of our nation hanging by a thread which Chu Ki-chul sensed with his prophetic imagination? It was not simply the Korean *minjung*'s political-economical and cultural-linguistic subordination to Japanese imperialism. What was more threatening and horrible for Chu Ki-chul was falling prey to Japanese idolatry. In our times of the resurgence of Japanese ultranationalism as well as rearmament, it is the calling of God for the Korean church to struggle against not only the old Japanese idolatry of 'wealthy nation strong army' under the system of imperial absolutism, but also the new form of idolatry internalized in the Korean people, namely, 'econo-animalism' and mammonism. The last part of Chu Ki-chul's sermon became a prophecy envisioning the fruit of his martyrdom in the newly liberated and independent nation.

> Climbing Mount Nebo and looking over Canaan,
> it is the hundred year long expected land beyond the Jordan.
> Though I cannot enter it, I lay my body over this mountain,
> My body offered to God is the sacrifice at the altar.
> My body given to compatriots has been worn out for a hundred years.
> Brothers and sisters, please don't worship idols when you get there.
> May my compatriots enjoy blessed life in the promised land.

2. Sonbi (Scholar) Spirit and the Korean Church

Where is the wise man? Where is the *sonbi*? (1 Corinthians 1:20).

If England is proud of its gentlemanliness, America its frontier spirit, and Japan its samurai spirit (Bushido), then Korea is proud of its *sonbi* (scholar) spirit. The *sonbi* spirit has survived the five centuries of the Chosun dynasty in which Confucianism was the dominant ideology.[14] One of the most typical *sonbi*s was Cho Kwang-cho (1482-1519) who was the leader of a short-lived reform and a victim of *sawha* (a purge of literati). He was the model of a true *sonbi* who lived and died for the sake of righteousness and chastity. A true *sonbi* is a human being who can clearly distinguish righteousness from interest, public life from privacy. Following his teacher Kim Koengpil, who was an example of keeping the principles of righteousness for self-cultivation, Cho Kwang-cho became the model of a true *sonbi* striving to serve in public life on the basis of self-cultivation. The *sonbi* spirit teaches people what they should be ashamed of and teaches them to seek public righteousness instead of private interest. The title of *sonbi* is not confined to its original meaning, Confucian scholar. Instead it is widely applied to the naming of everyone who lives and dies for nation and people. Ahn Joong-keun (1879-1910), who shot and killed Marquis Ito, the mastermind of Japanese colonialization of Korea, and was later executed by the Japanese imperialists, was called 'righteous *sonbi*'. One of his autographic maxims, "When you find interest, think of righteousness; when you meet danger, give your life," most succinctly tells about true *sonbi* spirit.

Chu Ki-chul was a righteous *sonbi* for the kingdom of God. His understanding of righteousness is Confucian in its ethos though it was firmly grounded theologically on Paul's and the Reformers' doctrine of justification. One of the parts of his last sermon is "Grant me to live and to die for righteousness" which consists of three points. First, the *sonbis'* righteousness of loyalty to the nation is related to Christian righteousness; second, Korean women's righteousness of chastity for their husbands is related to Christian righteousness; third, Chu Ki-chul confesses his righteousness of loyalty to the kingdom of God and chastity for Christ.

> Every one born in the world has righteousness which he as a human being should achieve. As a subject, one is expected to achieve the righteousness of loyalty; as a woman, the righteousness of chastity; as a Christian, Christian righteousness.[15]

The biblical meaning of righteousness, which Chu Ki-chul calls Christian righteousness, is derived from the context of the righteous' suffering in the Old Testament and of martyrdom in the New Testament. According to the prophet Habakkuk, "the righteous shall live by his faith" (Habakkuk 2: 4). Here faith means faithfulness, moral steadfastness, trustworthiness, and loyalty to Yahweh and his covenant. Especially in the Gospel of Matthew, the Old Testament understanding of righteousness is related to Jesus' message of the kingdom. The essence of the Law and the Prophets is "the kingdom and its righteousness" (Matthew 6: 33). Since the community in the Gospel of Matthew was in a situation of martyrdom, it is no wonder that Jesus, in the Gospel of Matthew, clearly distinguished prophetic righteousness from pharisaic righteousness, and he constantly exhorted his disciples to seek the former.

> Blessed are those who are persecuted because of righteousness, for theirs
> is the Kingdom of God. . . . For I tell you that unless your righteousness

surpasses that of the Pharisees and the teachers of the law, you will certainly not enter the Kingdom of God. (Matthew 5: 10, 20)

Jesus criticizes pharisaic righteousness because it is not righteousness for the kingdom of God but self-righteousness. It is misleading to understanding the Confucian ethos of righteousness as an analogy for pharisaic righteousness. A Confucianist can, of course, become self-righteous and hypocritical as much as any Christian can. Confucian righteousness should instead be interpreted as an analogy for prophetic righteousness. The *sonbi* spirit refers to the spirit of a human being who gives his or her life to save the lives of others. It is the "freedom of the heart for others" (Barth). Such expressions as "a man of the principle of righteousness," "a righteous man," and "a righteous *sonbi*" do not mean a pharisaic, self-righteous, and hypocritical man. To the contrary, it means a prophetic, self-sacrificing, and sincere man. In his last sermon, Chu Ki-chul quoted the famous poem of Chung Mong-ju, the fifteenth century Confucian *sonbi* who gave his life for the dying Koryu dynasty.

> This body dying, dying again for a hundred times again
> The white skeleton turning to ash, the soul dispersing
> A crimson heart for my lover will never stop beating.

The climax of the poem lies in "a crimson heart" which is the heart broken by the tragic collapsing of the power and authority of his king and the dynasty. Such a crimson heart is the clue to the righteousness of loyalty and chastity for the nation. Chu exclaimed, "Being a Christian, a crimson heart for my Lord will never stop beating! Dying and dying again for ten or a hundred times again, the great righteousness and chastity for my Lord will never change." It is significant to note that Chu Ki-chul not merely broadens the range of the righteousness of loyalty and chastity involved in the husband-wife relation and the king-subject relation but also transforms it into the righteousness of loyalty and chastity for the kingdom of God and the Lord. However, it is more significant to notice that Chu Ki-chul's wisdom and power of spiritual discernment in the age of idolatry comes from the seemingly exclusive theology of righteousness which grew out of an openness to the indigenous spirituality and ethos. Origen, whose father was a martyr, considered martyrdom the supreme achievement of the Christian life. In his "Exhortation to Martyrdom," Origen interprets the meaning of "a jealous God" in the Old Testament in terms of the husband-wife relation. According to Origen, the passage "For the Lord tempts you to know whether you love the Lord your God with all your heart and with all your soul" (Deuteronomy 13:3-4) illuminates the God of love and grace who uses jealousy to keep us from idolatry.

> In my opinion just as the husband who is concerned to help his bride to live chastely, to bring all her affection towards her husband and to take every precaution to avoid another man, if he is wise, will show some jealousy and will adopt this attitude to his bride, as a precautionary remedy: so also the Lawgiver (especially if it be clear that he is "the firstborn of all creation") says to the soul betrothed to God that he is jealous. His purpose is to separate the hearers from all fornication with demons and with the supposed gods. It is as a jealous God that he says of those who have in any way gone a-whoring after other gods: "They provoked me to jealousy against that which is not God, they made me wrathful against their idols. And I will provoke them to jealousy with people who are not a nation, I will make them wrathful against a foolish nation. For the fire is kindled from my anger, and it shall burn to the bottom of Hades" (Deuteronomy 32:21-22).[16]

As for Origen, faith in the jealous God is not exclusive subordination to a despotic god but liberation from idols and false gods. For Chu Ki-chul, faith in the loving yet utterly unapproachable God is a precaution against demons and false gods. According to Chu Ki-chul, "Talking about the love of God without mentioning of the righteousness and holiness of God is the deception of demons" because "love which lacks righteousness and truth is not true love" and "love is not rude, love does not delight in evil but rejoices with the truth" (1 Corinthians 13: 5-6). The notion of the jealousy and wrath of God is the antidote against false pluralism as well as sentimental love. Such a notion demands that we love God passionately with 'a crimson heart': "Love your God with all your heart and with all your soul and with all your strength." (Deuteronomy 6:5)

> To the cross, to the cross, to the cross that the Lord bore I offer my body. How many days does our life like dew on the grass continue? Life is short, but righteousness is eternal. My beloved brothers and sisters, let's live with righteousness and die with righteousness. Life abandoning righteousness, even righteousness for Jesus, is inferior to the life of a dog or any other beasts. Jesus is alive. Let's live with Jesus and die with Jesus.[17]

For Chu Ki-chul righteousness is not pharisaic self-righteousness but righteousness which is imputed and imparted by the righteousness of Christ. The Confucian ethos of loyalty and chastity implies 'a crimson heart' as the locus of prevenient grace to receive the imputed and imparted righteousness of Christ. Shame is overcome only by "Christ's blood and righteousness, that is my adornment and my fine raiment" (Luther). Chu Ki-chul says, "Initially we bear the cross, but later the cross of the Lord bears us." Appropriating the *sonbi* spirit of 'a crimson heart' for a Korean Christian understanding of righteousness, Chu Ki-chul's faith of *il-saghakoh* contributed to the kind of theology of the Spirit that fights against idolatry. Such theology of the Spirit is effective in discerning spirits, whether they are of true love or of sentimental love, whether they are of true righteousness or of self-righteousness. Kosuke Koyama points out that the essence of Japanese idolatry, self-righteousness, was caused by a parochial god.

> Self-righteousness is the source of parochialism. All nations are self-right-eous. All nations are, in this fundamental sense, parochial. The concept of self-righteousness must not be confined to religious dimensions. Human behavior in education, politics, economics, international relations and mili-tary preparations is shot through with self-righteousness, though we are remarkably clever at camouflaging it to appear otherwise. The inner emotion of self-righteousness expresses itself outwardly in the form of imperialism. Self-righteousness frees the nation's imperial propensities but it paralyses the nation's ability to make moral judgment, particularly in the area of her international relations. The Japanese gods told us, during the war, that the difference between Japan and China was that Japan told the truth and China told lies. It also declared repeatedly that evil emanates from the United States and good has its homeland in Japan. Our moral judgment crippled by self-righteousness, we were free to turn our energy to imperialism. It is a peculiar component of human tragedy that a paralyzed morality can produce such enormous spiritual energy in the service of the demonic.[18]

When the name of Jesus Christ and that of the Japanese emperor came into conflict, most of Korean church shamefully submitted themselves to the deception and threat of the Japanese government which defined Shintoism not as a religion but as a national custom. Nevertheless, God reserved two thousand Christians (fifty pastors among them) in the Korean church--all whose knees had not bowed down to Amaterasu Ohmikami (the Japanese solar goddess). If the righteous *sonbi*s of the Chosun dynasty, who were for public righteousness and against private interest, were persecuted and killed, the Korean Christians, who rejected emperor wor-ship, were imprisoned and martyred for the sake of the kingdom of God. Chu Ki-chul's struggle against Japanese idolatry should not belong to past history because the idolatry of the Japanese sun goddess has been resurging in East Asia in a more subtle way than before, I. e., not in the overtly militaristic way but in the covertly neo-colonialistic way. The new idolatry of the 'JapaNies' (Japan and Newly industrializing east Asian countries such as Korea, Taiwan, Hong Kong, and Singapore) is 'econo-animalism' which seeks economic interest at all cost.

The theological situation of the post-Chu Ki-chul Korean church is similar to that of Origen's burning sublimation of martyrdom. Our struggle against the new idolatry demands an enormous ethical and spiritual self-denial combined with a keen intellectual openness in our religiously pluralistic age. This asks for a new paradigmatic change in doing theology in Asia as well as in Korea. As Kenneth Surin points out, the so-called theology of religious pluralism which belongs to Western liberal religious thought is parochial. As long as the theological issues concerning religious pluralism "did nothing to address the situation of those who are starving, they functioned as ideological cover for a status quo that is hostile to the Kingdom of God."[19] Therefore, Tom. F. Driver has a point when he says, "In order to protect itself against elitism and complacency, the pluralist cause must come to see that particular religions are delivered from idolatry not only by reflection upon 'otherness' and diversity but also by commitment and action in behalf of the poor."[20] As Chu Ki-chul appropriated the Confucian ethos of the *sonbi* spirit in order to struggle against the Japanese idolatry of emperor worship, Korean theology of the Spirit needs to dialogue with and to learn from people of other faiths, such as Buddhists, as well as Confucianists in order to overcome a false pluralism that tolerates the new idolatry of mammonism.

Where is the wise man or the *sonbi* who is not for this world but for the kingdom of God? Does the image of pastor as the *sonbi* for the kingdom of God, who teaches and persuades his or her congregation to discern ethically and spiritually shame and righteousness, still remain in the Korean church? In our time of globalization and limitless competition, the new idolatries of 'econo-animalism" and mammonism are injuring many fathers laid off in the name of honorary retirement for the sake of strengthening the competitiveness of business and of the nation state. Is the Korean church healing their broken heart by experiencing shame instead of honor? How long is the Korean church going to be intoxicated with belief in material blessings and the myth of numerical church growth? Is not the healing ministry of the Korean church for the broken hearted failing because it bypasses or lets them bypass shame? Of course, no patriarchal authorities should be allowed at home, in church, at school, or in society. However, genuine authority is possible only when one faces the bypassed shame and his broken heart is healed. Jesus Christ, who was the Lord and yet became a servant, shows us the new paradigm of genuine authority. *Soyang* (Jesus' sheep) Chu Ki-chul, who rejected idolatry and did not lose 'a crimson heart' of righteousness and chastity for Christ, even in utmost helplessness and shame, has provided the image of a father and pastor who looks after the Lord and who became a servant.

"The Road Outside the Camp," a hymn Chu Ki-chul wrote in the midst of severe and cruel torture, is still inspiring us to seek the way of the true father and true pastor. The first and second verses are in praise of the Passion of Christ, and the remaining three verses are about Christian discipleship which follows in Jesus" footsteps. At the end of the third verse the narrow road outside the camp turns into an uphill pass. Why? It is because Chu Ki-chul, righteous *sonbi* for the kingdom of God, went with the Lord over the hill of Arirang, over which so many righteous *sonbi*s for the nation and the *minjung* had also gone. The hymn has been sung to the tune of "The Blue Danube Waltz." The time has come for us to get rid of the frivolous rhythm of the Western bourgeoisie and to sing and dance to the tune of Arirang. This must be a matter of the authentic indigenization of Christian hymns. Through such 'Arirangization' of "The Road Outside the Camp," the Holy Spirit turns the hill of Arirang full of *han* and shame into the hill of Golgotha, the hill of calling and rapture. Those who have been ashamed of "my lover leaving and going away" and embraced the *han* of "a swollen foot" in the depth of a broken heart receive new eyes to discover the way of eternal life from the Spirit "covering a hurt leg and curing a lamed leg," responding courageously to the call of God by singing "Let even me go over the high hill of Golgotha!"

> *Arirang, Arirang, Araryo!* Going over the hill of *Arirang*
> My lover leaving and going away
> Will have a swollen foot within 10 *li*.
>
> *Arirang, Arirang, Araryo!* Going over the hill of *Arirang*
> Without tears and blood no one can go
> To narrow road outside the camp.
>
> *Arirang, Arirang, Araryo!* Going over the hill of *Arirang*
> I must tread this road for eternal blessing
> Even in hunger and death I will climb up.
>
> *Arirang, Arirang, Araryo!* Going over the hill of *Arirang*
> Cover my hurt leg, cure my lamed leg
> Let me stand firm and bear my cross.

> *Arirang, Arirang, Araryo!* Going over the hill of *Arirang*
> Open my closed eyes to see the Way
> Let me go over the hill of Golgotha.

1) Chu Ki-chul, "Five themes of my prayer," in Kim Jonah, *Ilsaghakoh* (Seoul: Faith & Love, 1994), pp. 255-256.

2) Quoted from Kim Heup-young, "The study of Confucianism as a theological task," KAATS, *Korea Journal of Theology*, Vol. 1, 1995, p. 260.

3) *Ibid.*

4) Min Kyung-bae, *The Rev. Martyr Chu Ki-chul* (Seoul: Korea Christian Publishing Company, 1985), pp. 18-19.

5) Cf. Walter T. Davis, "Shame and pastoral care", unpublished paper presented at The 2nd International Consultation on Practical Theology, Nae Jang San. Korea, Oct. 18-20, 1993.

6) Cf. James Fowler, "Shame: Toward a practical theological understanding," *The Christian Century*, Aug. 25-Sept. 1, 1993: 816-819.

7) Chu Ki-chul, "The second coming of the Lord," in Min Kyung-bae, *op. cit.*, p. 302.

8) Chu Ki-chul, "Contemplation on suffering." in Kim Jonah, *op. cit.*, p. 257.

9) D. Bonhoeffer, *Ethics* (N. Y.: Macmillian Publishing Co., 1978), p. 20, p. 24.

10) Karl Barth, *Church Dogmatics,* Vol., III, 1, p. 279.

11) Karl Barth, *Church Dogmatics,* Vol., IV, 3.1, p. 120.

12) *Ibid.*, p. 127.

13) Chu Ki-chul, "One hundred and twenty year long life of Moses," in Min Kyung-bae, *op. cit.*, pp. 167-170.

14) Cf. Yun Sa-soon, *Confucian Thought in Korea* (Seoul: Yeoreumsa, 1988).

15) Chu Ki-chul, "Five themes of my prayer," in Kim Jonah, *op. cit.*, p. 261.

16) Origen, "Exhortation to Martyrdom," in *The Library of Christian Classics: Alexandrian Christianity!* (Philadelphia: The Westminister Press), pp. 398-399.

17) Chu Ki-chul, "Five themes of my prayer," in Kim Jonah, *op. cit.*, p. 263.

18) Kosuke Koyama, *Mount Fuji and Mount Sinai* (N.Y.: Orbis, 1984), pp. 23-24.

19) Cf. John Hick and Paul Knitter, ed., *The Myth of Christian Uniqueness* (New York: Orbis, 1987), p. 205.

20) *Ibid.*, p. 217.

CHAPTER 7

Theology of the Spirit and Theology of Life

1. Three beat salvation: the message of the full gospel

THE POST-KOREAN WAR Holy Spirit movement can hardly be understood unless we take into consideration the darkness death caused by the civil war in the land of suffering which was brutally colonialized by Japan. The Korean *minjung*'s groans and thirst for abundant life became important issues even in the religious realm. In the totally destroyed situation it was no wonder that the first priority of survival was combined with religious enthusiasm. But the religious enthusiasm demonstrated an urgency that could not be satisfied with any glorious afterlife as a means of escape from the impoverished conditions of the post-war society. Such an otherworldly message as "Believe in Jesus to go to heaven!" did not appeal to the Korean people any more because they found themselves already in hell in reality and were not afraid of real hell. Unless they experienced real heaven on earth they could hardly be persuaded by the Gospel.

The Holy Spirit movement of the Rev. Cho Yong-gi (1936-), which began in 1958 when the scar of war still remained everywhere, started with helping the poor and sick people taste the abundant life in the power of the Spirit. Cho Yong-gi's message, which he himself calls three-beat salvation, has a strongly this-worldly orientation, for it combines the salvation of the soul with material blessing and physical healing in order to convert the poor and starving people. Cho describes what he discovered when he began his ministry;

> The poor people of our village were not interested in heaven and hell. They were only concerned with what they shall eat tomorrow for they were tired of their dayfly-like life. They had no time and energy to plan for future.

91

Every home I visited had the same wish to solve the problem of the necessities of life.[1]

Cho's Holy Spirit movement, which caused the miraculous growth of the Full Gospel Central Church, should be differentiated from the church growth movement in the 1970s. The main force in the early development of the full gospel movement was the urban poor who moved from rural areas. But the main target of the church growth movement in the 1970s was the middle class which appeared with increasing economic development. As the church growth movement became dominant in the churches of the middle class, the Shamanistic tendency of the full gospel movement was overcome by the American form of pentecostalism. There has been no other Korean church like the Full Gospel Central Church whose growth in connection with pentecostalism has become the center of worldwide attention. There has been no other church like the Full Gospel Central Church whose problems in theology have brought about the conflict between economic value and the value of life.

The theological core of the full gospel movement lies in its understanding of the Holy Spirit as a personal and maternal image. To call the Holy Spirit *sungryungnim* in Korean and to attend to *nim* (reverend person) is unusual in the tradition of Western Christianity. According to the Korean Shamanistic tradition, it is common sense to attend to *shin-ryungnim* (divine spirit as revered person). The place of the Holy Spirit in Cho's ministry and theology is almost absolute. Without communion with the Holy Spirit, communion with neither the Father nor the Son is possible. Cho describes his special relationship with the Holy Spirit as follows;

> Nowadays I always force myself to recognize the Holy Spirit, to welcome the Holy Spirit and to worship the Holy Spirit, because He is a person. Every time before I go out to preach, I always say, 'Dear Holy Spirit, I welcome you. I recognize you and I love you. I depend upon you. Dear Holy Spirit, let's go! Let's bring the glory of God to the people![2]

The orthodox doctrine of the Trinity affirms the personality of the Holy Spirit. But Cho goes even further to claim to attend to the Holy Spirit within one's heart. Of course, the Bible also teaches us the indwelling of the Holy Spirit in the believer's heart. And such indwelling is always conditioned by the rest of the persons in the Trinity. But Cho asserts direct communion with the Holy Spirit, which is very Korean as well as Shamanistic. Cho's expressions, such as "Dear Holy Spirit, we did a wonderful job together" or "I try to float on the wave of the Holy Spirit," are typical of Shamanistic pentecostalism in Korea.

The center of *kut* (shaman ritual) is *kongsu* (message from divine spirits). According to Kim Kum-wha, national Shaman, "*Shinryungnim* (divine spirit) is dignified yet affectionate and full of love. If shaman's attitude toward people is tough and fearful, she cannot help them. When shaman has dialogue with *shinryungnim*, she has to approach with open and true heart. *Kongsu* is central in *kut*. *Kongsu* is not created by shaman, it is rather the words and heart bestowed on people by gods who help them. Shaman always talks with *shinryungnim* closely to receive good *kongsu*. Shaman also has to know human affairs in order to deliver *kongsu* truthfully. *Kut* is of no use unless shaman plays the role of mediator between gods and people very well."[3] The relationship between the full gospel movement and Shamanism is deeper than the fact that both of them are religions of blessing. Cho's understanding of the word of God reflects the traits of Christianized *kongsu*.

Cho divides the word of God into two categories, i.e., *logos* and *rhema*. *Logos* is the general, intellectual, and static word. *Rhema* is the dynamic and powerful word which is bestowed on a specific person as the voice of God in his or her heart. The distinction between *logos* and *rhema* is very crucial in Cho's ministry and theology. It reminds us of the 'inner word" of spiritualism in the period of the Reformation as well as in the Middle Ages. According to the theological report of the Korean Presbyterian Church on the Full Gospel Central Church, "Pastor Cho David (Yong-gi) is unbiblical because Jesus as *logos* performed miracles with the power of *logos* (Matthew 8:16) and he himself was *logos* (John 1:1-14)." After the theological debate with the Presbyterian Church, Cho's opinion of *rhema* did not change in substance except that the neoorthodox distinction between the written word of God and the proclaimed word of God was borrowed to express the distinction between *logos* and *rhema*. This change in expression not in substance might have soothed the conflict between the Full Gospel Church and the mainline Protestant denominations, but it harmed Cho's theological consistency.

Cho's ministry and theology has been centered around the Holy Spirit and religious experience in comparison with the Bible-centered theology of the mainline churches. However, Cho's recent theology, which has been systematized by the International Institute of Theology at the Full Gospel Central Church, reflects not only the maturity of harmony and balance but also a setback caused by the routinization of his charismatic power. Compared to the early Cho's pneumacentric theology of divine-human participation and his ministry based on maternal spirituality, his recent theology leans toward divine sovereignty and his recent ministry reflects masculine spirituality. It has something to do with the change from the early ministry of healing, that helped the groaning and dying souls survive the post-war despair, to his later ministry of blessing, that guaranteed the material wealth and secular success of those living in an era of economic development. Cho's ministry of healing and his ministry of blessing have been closely related to each other. Cho's positive message did contribute greatly to the transition from the desperate situation of death to the hope of abundant life in the overall process of upward class mobility during the Korean economic boom. Cho speaks of the creative power of the word (*rhema*) of God as follows:

> Koreans habitually say, 'I'm dying.' 'I'm dying because it's too hot. I'm dying because my stomach is full. I'm dying because I'm happy. I'm dying because I'm afraid.' . . . From now on let's throw negative words away and let's get used to speak positive words. Your language has to change first before you change yourself. . . . From whom can we learn such new language? We can learn the most wonderful language from the Bible. We have to let the Holy Spirit rejuvenate us through the adequate words in the Bible and work in the heart of each one of us.[4]

Cho's theology of *rhema* does not stop short at interpreting the meaning of the Bible. It goes even further to bring about certain consequences by means of an act of speech led by the Holy Spirit and grounded in the Bible. The preaching of the word of God in mainline Korean Protestant churches is based on the interpretation of the word by the preacher who acts as a spokesman for God. But Cho is not satisfied with it. He discovered that the strong desire of the Holy Spirit working within him made him not merely interpret the word of God but also creatively use the word for the sake of believers thirsting for healing. Cho describes his own experience of the exhorting words of the Holy Spirit;

> Don't beg for gift or pray for healing only. Since the Holy Spirit is present in your worship, you must proclaim the word of God. Give me a chance to perform miracles. In the beginning when I created the world, I proclaimed, "Let there be light," then there was light. When I also proclaimed, "Let there be firmament," then there was firmament. In the same way I put the word of faith into your mouth and the Spirit is present in your worship. Speak such words as "Be healed in the name of Jesus Christ!" "Go away, cancer, in the name of Jesus Christ!" The word of God and the Holy Spirit are working with us![5]

94

To speak creative language in the power of the Holy Spirit is to become God's partner in creation as well as in the salvific work of Jesus Christ. "We have to learn how to proclaim the word of command as Jesus did." We can learn it only when "the Holy Spirit applies the word spoken by God to the heart of people so that the word becomes the 'word God is speaking right now.'" Cho suggests five steps of receiving *rhema*. Fasting prayer is the first step; to have holy desires aroused by the Holy Spirit is the second step; to verify the word according to the Bible is the third step; to discover an evidence as a sign is the fourth step; to grasp a sacred moment is the fifth step. At the last step, when one waits in prayer to know a time fitting for the will of God, one is again connected with the first step. How long should one wait for God? Cho tries to answer this question with his typical eloquence and persuasive power.

> If your heart is anxious even after you pray, it means time is not ready. It indicates red light is on. Pray continuously and wait. When red light is off and green light is on, true peace will surge into your heart. Then, don't hesitate to get up immediately to start. Run with the highest speed and with blessing and *rhema* in your heart. The miracle of God will follow you one after another.[6]

In his study of pentecostal spirituality Harvey Cox includes Cho's full gospel movement under the title of "Shamans and Entrepreneurs: Primal Spirituality on the Asian Rim." Cox argues that pentecostalism in Korea could incorporate many of the characteristics of Shamanism and also prepare people remarkably well for modern political and economic survival. Cox considers Cho's pentecostalism "Christian Shamanism" because he finds that it is helping people recover vital elements in their culture that are threatened by modernization. Such vital elements of Shamanism as ecstatic trances, demon possession, and exorcism, all seem to find their place in the worship of *Hananim,* the name Korean Christians call God. Cox observes Korean pentecostalism in terms of a spectacular example of the fusion of the old-fashioned or possibly superstitious practice of Shamanic exorcism and a certifiably up-to-date religion, one that came from the most up-to-date of all countries, the United States. Cox also finds a certain element of Shamanism coherent with Christianity.

> Shamanism is based on the premise that neither human beings nor nature itself hold the ultimate power in the universe. The ultimate power is a divine one. Further, it holds that the divine power can be brought to bear positively on earthly sorrow and pain, and that human beings

95

need not be inert recipients of fate but can take measures that will improve their situation.[8]

The typical example for the above statement in Shamanism is *Jae-sukut* (a Shamanic ritual for material blessing). *Jaesukut* is not so much a ritual for material blessing as a ritual for the recovery of harmony among humanity, nature, and gods. Only when such harmony is recovered is blessing possible. In ordinary use of *jaesu* in Korean it refers to "good luck in money, health and long life," but its original meaning is "ultimate salvation realized by a new harmony recovered through eliminating disharmony."[8] The symbol for the primordial form of Korean Shamanism is three-color *taichi* (*ying-yang*) which was used as an emblem of the 1988 Seoul Olympics. Unlike the Chinese *taichi* symbol which consists of two colors, the Korean *taichi* symbol has the three primary colors indicating the harmony of heaven, earth, and humanity. The three color *taichi* symbol is also identified in the most typical beat in Korean traditional music, namely, *semachi* rhythm. For instance, Arirang has *semachi* rhythm. The accent in such Korean rhythm always lies in the first beat, thus the first syllable of Arirang, *Ar*, has a strong accent. You never begin singing Arirang with a soft beat in crescendo. You must sing it with a strong beat in decrescendo.

Cox does not notice Cho's creative theologizing which makes the fusion of Christianity and Shamanism possible. The so-called three-beat salvation is the essence of Cho's theology. The metaphor of three-beat salvation comes from his imaginative interpretation of the most important *rhema* in his ministry and theology, i.e. 3 John 2: "Dear friend, I pray that you may enjoy good health and that all may go well with you, even as your soul is getting along well."

Cho creatively violates the text of prayer in order to envision three-beat salvation as the message of total salvation-- salvation not only of soul but also of environment and of body. Thus, three-beat salvation means material blessing and physical health as well as salvation of soul. Of course, Cho also emphasizes that the accent is on the first part of salvation, namely, salvation of the soul, not in separation from the rest of the beats but in close connection with them. Only when one's relationship with the good God who created heaven and earth and reigns in the world is recovered, can material blessing and physical health be given to him or her. Cho boldly asserts, "Today, believers in Jesus have great responsibility. It is to live a rich life. If we are poor without a special reason, it is an insult for Jesus."

2. The Fourth Dimension: Beyond Full Gospel

The problem of the Full Gospel lies in its magical understanding of the atonement of Jesus. The message of three-beat salvation tends to remain a childish spirituality avoiding Christian discipleship and responsibility. Once you come to enjoy material blessing and physical health, such a message can hardly maintain its appealing and persuasive power. The recent slowdown of the growth of the Full Gospel Central Church was predictable. In the past most of the congregation of the Full Gospel Central Church were the urban poor. Now they have become middle-class citizens whose spiritual needs are more sophisticated than before. In Cho's book *The Fourth Dimension,* which was written in 1979 in English and recently translated into Korean, there is no mention of three-beat salvation. Instead, Cho says, "Silver and gold I don't have. Food, rice and clothes I don't have. Therefore, I have nothing to give you. But I can give you a thing which is the most precious in the world. It is the fact that God dwells in every believer."

Cho considers the New Age movement the strongest challenge to his full gospel movement. He calls it Oriental mysticism and claims that its leaders inspect the spiritual world of Satan and enter into it to perform miracles of healing by their own faith. Oriental mysticism also belongs to the fourth dimension, the spiritual world in opposition to the material world which is three dimensional. Cho argues that Christ and Satan are in conflict in the spiritual world. He also believes that transcendental meditation and Buddhist mysticism, which are swaying the whole world, belong to a Satanic effort to develop merely the potentiality of the human mind (psyche). Cho criticizes any contemporary Christian faith and theology which cannot produce miracles because they stop at being mere words and theory. Cho's pentecostal movement also contributed to the development of the potential power of the human psyche in its own way. It is not Christian to judge others while they are doing similar things. Cho's direct equation of the gospel with miraculous effects tends to reduce the gospel to a pentecostal New Age movement. Cho's suggestion of dreams and visions by using the language of the Holy Spirit is hardly distinguishable from mind control or mind expansion. Cho defines a miracle as the great salvific change from death to new life. A miracle for Cho is pragmatic as well as supernatural. Since the fourth dimension of the Holy Spirit dominates and rules the three-dimensional material world, through the fourth dimension Christians can command their lives and environment to produce miracles in the name of Jesus Christ. He calls such commands the language of the Holy Spirit.

> If the Holy Spirit gives you faith that can move a mountain, don't beg Him to move it. Rather, command as following, "You, mountain! Move to that sea!" Then, amazing things will appear.[9]

Cho's command language of the Holy Spirit resembles both ancient magic and modern technical manipulation. It is so attached to an immediate solution of problems that it loses sight of the person's location in his or her social, political, and economic context. The person who has competence of the language of the Holy Spirit seems to have a certain illusion of control over his or her own life and environment. Suppose a Christian businessman faces a problem in his business. If he onesidedly commands that the problem be solved without considering his relationship with other businessmen, consumers, and laborers in his own socioeconomic structure, it must be unethical and contrary to the gospel. Such spirituality cannot help but serve the capitalist system of money and power. And the life-world which Cho calls life and environment becomes colonialized by the magico-technical discourse of command and manipulation. Emphasizing that more than seventy percent of Jesus' activity was performing miracles, Cho tries to explain Jesus' healing miracles in terms of the magico-technical discourse of domination and control. Jesus' act of healing, however, was not a strategic act of showing his power in order to surprise and dominate the *minjung,* but communicative praxis to help those who needed healing and salvation to return to their social relations as new beings. The focus of Jesus' healing is not merely on the healing of sick persons but on the restoration of their rights in their life-world. A direct imitation of Jesus' act of physical healing cannot help but fall into magic which has nothing to do with Jesus' original intention for *missio Dei.*

Cho used to accuse pastors and theologians of the mainline Protestant churches of losing the vital power of the Gospel because they do not witness to the blood of Jesus. Instead they speak of the life, teaching, and moral truth of Jesus. Cho tends to confuse salvation with discipleship. Jesus' bearing the cross does not make Christians' bearing their own cross unnecessary. Not only belief in the cross of Jesus but also following Jesus by bearing one's own cross is the core of Christian spirituality. Cho's quasi-dispensationalist understanding of the Holy Spirit weakens the meaning of the cross of Jesus in the Christian life. Cho's favorite text on the Holy Spirit is John 14:26: "But the Counselor, the Holy Spirit, whom the Father will send in my name, will teach you all things and will remind you of everything I have said to you." For Cho the Counselor, the Holy Spirit is the real agent of Jesus here and now. The Holy Spirit is the most central person in the Holy Trinity in the present era of the pentecostal movement. Cho confesses:

> Dear Holy Spirit, Jesus is now at the right hand of God. Right now, dear Holy Spirit, you are the one who is with me. You are God, the agent of the love of Jesus, the one who is working with me in this place. You are my senior pastor and counselor. I have neglected and mistreated you. I have tried to control you and to consider you a mystical power. Please, forgive me.[10]

Cho claims that his striking experience of direct and free communion with the Holy Spirit is based on 2 Corinthians 13:13: "May the grace of the Lord Jesus Christ, and the love of God, and the fellowship of the Holy Spirit be with you all." Cho interprets this text as follows:

> Greek word *koinonia* means 'fellowship' or 'communion.' We have to have direct communion with the Holy Spirit in order to have koinonia with the Holy Spirit. It is absurd to have indirect dialogue in order to have fellowship with someone. "Hi, I love you, how is your family?" Like this, we need direct talk. . . . The Holy Spirit and I are one, and I have been living constantly in the Holy Spirit.[11]

Cho's claim that we have to have direct communion with the Holy Spirit because Jesus sits at the right hand of God is far from the meaning of the trinitarian spirituality of 2 Cor. 13:13. Jesus' sitting at the right hand of God does not mean he is absent from earth. It means his present reign is authorized by God the Father. The communion with the Holy Spirit is conditioned by the grace of Jesus Christ and the love of God. In other words, the primary meaning of the communion of the Holy Spirit lies in the Holy Trinity. In 1997 the Korean Orthodox Church became a member church of the National Council of Churches in Korea. The Orthodox understanding of the Holy Trinity is helpful for the correction of the quasi-dispensationalist understanding of the Holy Spirit in pentecostalism.

A famous icon of the Holy Trinity drawn by a Russian Orthodox artist in the fifteenth century is a wonderful symbol for opening up the deep meaning of the trinitarian doctrine of the Holy Spirit. The motif of the icon is based on the story of the three visitors from God who came to Abraham near the great trees of Mamre (Genesis 18). The three persons of the Trinity, Father, Son, and Holy Spirit, sit around the table from left to right in the icon. The chalice containing the blood of the Son is at the center of the communion table. The three persons of the Trinity do not have beards. They all look feminine and posed in gracefulness. The Son and the Holy Spirit turn their heads in the direction of the Father. The two fingers of the right hand of the Father point to the chalice, the two fingers of the right hand of the Son point to the Holy Spirit, and the palm of the right hand of the Holy Spirit is about to move as if it were ready to lay on the suffering creation. The first and foremost meaning the icon opens up is that the Holy Trinity is now at work in the world. A building and a tree behind the three persons in the icon symbolize that nature and history are embraced in the economy of God the Savior. Another crucial meaning the icon opens up is the communion of the Holy Trinity around the chalice. The communion of the Holy Spirit is communion within and among the Trinity before it becomes the communion of saints in the community of faith. Thus the meaning of the communion of the Holy Spirit presupposes the grace of the Son and the love of the Father. Without noticing the eternal communion of the Holy Trinity around the chalice containing the blood of Jesus Christ, Cho sees the shedding of the blood of Jesus Christ as the once and for all event in the history of salvation. Thus the direct communion of the Holy Spirit follows the Christ event. Direct communion with the Holy Spirit which is neither grounded on the love of God who gave the only Son nor mediated by the grace of Jesus Christ who shed his precious blood is not biblical or Christian.

An Orthodox metaphor for the close mutual communion and fellowship of the Holy Trinity is *perichoresis*, which means round dance. The three persons of the Trinity dance around the chalice on the communion table. Christians are invited to take part in the round dance of God the Father, God the Son, and God the Holy Spirit. The chalice of the precious blood of Christ is at the center of liturgical dance in Christian worship which celebrates trinitarian communion. Any dance which forgets or loses the chalice cannot become a part of Christian worship. Those pentecostal Christians who claim direct communion with the Holy Spirit love the Holy Spirit dance, but such a dance can easily fall victim to a religiously distorted form of eroticism. One must crawl with God before he or she dances in the Spirit! Isn't Cho's theology of the Holy Spirit a theology of glory *(theologia gloria)* because it prefers direct communion with the Holy Spirit, who descended after the Resurrection and Ascension of Christ, to sharing suffering and love with God who crawled in the cross of Jesus Christ? Can Cho's message of three-beat salvation console those who are in a situation of unbearable suffering, who fail in their lives and whose sicknesses are not cured, who experience meaninglessness and doubt whether they can continue to live, who are in a situation of theodicy, namely, a situation in which the justice of God is questioned?

In *Please, Say Just a Word,* written in desperate agony by Park Wan-suh, a well-known contemporary Korean novelist, after she lost her son, we can find more than mere literature, i.e., a confession of faith. When her fame as a novelist reached its peak, she lost her husband and son one after the other in 1988. Her son was a doctor in his twenties and was her only son besides her four daughters. In her great pain she cursed God, life, and herself. Night after night she drank beer, whisky, and *soja.* On the very first day that she went to a nearby convent for recuperation, she knelt down before a crucifix and cried out to God for a word for her. God kept silent. One day while she did not take notice of a nun's talk, all of sudden she thought to herself, "If I can change my mind from such resentment 'Why was my son taken away?' to 'Why can't be my son taken away?' I may find a clue for salvation." After she talked about how she lost her son with a woman who was visiting her sick daughter in the convent, she was so overwhelmed by pain and anger that she vomited in her bathroom. Holding onto a toilet stool while she vomited, she began to repent the sin emerging in her heart like a revelation.

> I have given nothing to others. No money, no love. Sharing freely my money and live is limited within a few of my family, relatives and friends. To the rest of others who can be called my neighbors I have been completely indifferent. . . . I realized that my complete indifference to others with whom I haven't given and taken was a great sin, thus, as the punishment for the sin I suffered the pain which would never disappear like a high mountain even though I would share it again and again with others. . . . At least for that moment it was the exact answer. And it was salvation. I will share even my pain if such sharing is worthy. . . . Lord, take me. Take my every freedom, my memory and intelligence, every will and everything I have and own. Even my pain. You have given all these things. Lord, I give them back to you. Everything is yours, deal with it just as you want. Give me your love and grace. It is enough for me.[12]

What did Park Wan-suh hear from God? Did God say a word to her? It was neither cheap grace nor an easy answer. God kept silent. Yet, through the merciful presence of the Holy Spirit groaning with her, words rose out of the depth of her being and struck her in the midst of great anxiety so powerfully that they helped her to a new state of life. Commenting on the literature of Park Wan-suh, a critic said, "Not healing wounds perfectly but living with and even attending on wounds is the destiny of all great writers. Literature is a form of attending on wounds." Every living being lives with wounds. Starting from her own wounds, Park Wan-suh could embrace the wounds of other people and of other living beings. This is the peak of maternal affection, the essence of the reverence for life and the beginning of true worship. It is not speculative theology but worship in spirit and truth that saves. Worship is a form of paying attention to the wounds of God.

> Crown Him the Lord of love; Behold His hands and side,
> Rich wounds, yet visible above, In beauty glorified;
> No angel in the sky can fully bear that sight.
> But downward bends His burning eyes at mysteries so bright. (M. Bridges)

Cho claims that Christ redeemed our sin, curse, and sickness so that we, as the heirs of God, inherit salvation, blessing, and health. But Cho forgets what St. Paul said: "Now if we are children, then we are heirs--heirs of God and co-heirs with Christ, if indeed we share in his sufferings in order that we may also share in his glory" (Romans 8: 17). Christians who welcome and have communion with the Holy Spirit do not escape sufferings but go through them. The Spirit of the crucified and resurrected Christ is the same Spirit groaning with the whole creation which is subjected to frustration and decay:

> We know that the whole creation has been groaning as in the pains of childbirth right up to the present time. Not only so, but we ourselves, who have the firstfruits of the Spirit, groan inwardly, as we wait eagerly for our adoption as sons, the redemption of our bodies. . . . In the same way, the Spirit helps us in our weakness. We do not know what we ought to pray, but the Spirit himself intercedes for us with groans that words cannot express (Romans 8:22, 23, 26).

What direction will the Holy Spirit movement of the Korean church have to take in the twenty-first century? It has to start with welcoming and attending to the Holy Spirit who is interceding for us with groans for the groaning creation. It has to aim at a genuinely evangelical and ecumenical spirituality that transforms those human beings who abuse nature, alienate their fellow humans out of their own greed, and worship their own success, health, and long life under the guise of the Holy Spirit movement, into new beings who take part in their fellow humans' sufferings, and embrace the groaning creation, and worship the wounds of God in trinitarian communion.

We are called not to be successful but to be faithful (Mother Teresa).

102

1) Cho Yong-gi, *The Fourth Dimension* (Seoul, 1996), p. 188.
2) Cho Yong-gi, *Successful Home Cell Groups* (Seoul, 1981), p. 124.
3) Kim Kum-wha, *Share your blessing, release your han* (Seoul, 1995), p. 58.
4) Cho, *The Fourth Dimension*, p. 91.
5) *Ibid.*, p. 94.
6) *Ibid.*, p. 132.
7) Harvey Cox, *Fire from Heaven* (Addison Wesley, 1995), pp. 227-228.
8) Cha Ok-soon, "Shamanism in Korean Christianity and the task of indigenization," Chang Sang and So Heung-ryul ed., *Doing theology with love* (Seoul, 1996), p. 314.
9) Cho, *The Fourth Dimension*, p. 96.
10) Cho, *A Secret of Church Growth* (Seoul, 1995), p. 251.
11) *Ibid.*, p. 252.

CHAPTER 8

Theology of the Spirit and Evangelical Ecumenism

1. A Flame of Love in the Midst of Suffering

REVEREND CHO WHA-SOON (1934-), who is the most promi nent representative of Korean Christian women and the unique leader guiding the direction of the Holy Spirit movement of the Korean church, was born and spent her childhood during Japanese colonial rule, committed her youth to the service of wounded soldiers in the Korean War, and witnessed to Christ with the farmers and laborers who were alienated and suffered in the process of economic development. When we interpret the history of the Holy Spirit movement in the Korean church we should be careful not to overestimate its bright and successful side on the one hand and leave out its dark side and failure on the other. Christian triumphalism is visible in every writing of church history. If we are deliberately oblivious of the events of divine judgment and human suffering, our relationship with other movements in national and *minjung* history will be tinctured with religious arrogance and Christian triumphal- ism. In the third period of the history of the Holy Spirit movement in the Korean church, Cho Wha-soon's story of the Urban Industrial Mission is a living witness to the presence of the Spirit of God. It is like a flame of love in the midst of suffering women laborers who were at the bottom of Korean society in the era of economic miracles.

Cho grew up in a typically conservative Christian family. Little Cho was of sensitive character. In her youth, together with her friends in church, she dreamt of serving the poor people in the countryside. The identity of her personality and the meaning and value of her life were formed by the spirit of love for others. While caring for severely wounded soldiers during the Korean War, she realized that she was called by God to do the hard work which the other people hesitated to do. Right after she graduated

104

from the Methodist seminary in Seoul, she was sent by her bishop to a deserted church in Dokjokdo, a small distant island. The Spirit of God led her into one of the poorest places in Korea. On the first Sunday in the church, she preached to just one person who was mentally retarded. Though she had been a conservative Christian attending early morning prayer every day, she had not had any extraordinary experience of the Holy Spirit until she was obliged to exorcize the evil spirit in a sick person. Through healing a possessed person, Cho developed the firm faith that together with God she could also overcome the demonic power of capitalism and mammonism later in her career. As pastor for a village church, Cho was quite successful. For instance, during her Dalwol church ministry, between 1963 and 1966, the membership increased from 20 to 150. That was one of the reasons why she could go back to the same church in 1983 after her eighteen-year industrial mission. Had she remained in her local church ministry, she might have become a successful minister or a great revivalist such as one often finds in the Korean church.

The amazing thing in Cho's life is that she has been always willing to leave for a new place whenever the Spirit of God called her. She realized that God had chosen a person who considered herself lacking. "Let the weak be strong" has been her most important motto throughout her whole life and career. Her decision to commit herself to the industrial mission in 1966 was a leap of faith. She obeyed the call of God to follow Jesus into the unknown future while deserting and even ruining her bright career as a successful woman minister. The place of Cho Wha-soon in the history of the Holy Spirit movement of the Korean church cannot be compared with anyone else because she is the only woman Christian and pastor who, with the help of the Spirit, acquired communicative competence in both evangelical and ecumenical praxis.[1] Of course, there have been many instances of linguistic competence in evangelical-ecumenical praxis within the male-dominated mission and theology. For instance, there have been so-called *minjung* theologians who merely theologize the *minjung* motif in intellectual categories which are not communicable to the real *minjung*. Cho's communicative competence has nothing to do with the fact that Cho is female (remember that most of the feminist theologians are not necessarily competent in communicating with women *minjung*). Instead it may come from her constant identification with the suffering women laborers. Acquiring such marvelous communicative competence must have required a very strenuous process in both Cho's life and the social biography of the laborers.

The fact that Cho's theology tends to subvert Western male-dominated theology seems to be similar to the position of Western feminist theology.

But its Third World and Korean *minjung* character justifies its treatment in Korean theology of the Spirit. The subjects of her theology were Korean women laborers. Her theology reflects three kinds of contradiction: nationality, gender, and class. Cho's tireless search for the presence of God among the Korean women laborers is well known. One day George Ogle, an American missionary who invited Cho to join the Inchon Industrial Mission, asked Cho to find God in the context of Dong-il Textile Company where Cho was placed to work for six months. Ogle even asked Cho to name God among the laborers. After experiencing confusion and inner struggle, Cho finally brought up the name of a young woman worker who was maltreated and considered a fool even by her fellow workers. This experience eventually made Cho break away from what she called the fake Christian faith. Cho's experience of such inversion was so intense and deep that she was changed to a different person. She became overwhelmed with prophetic indignation whenever the institutional church kept silent about the violations of human rights under Park's authoritarian bureaucratic regime. By naming God in such a shocking way, Cho's model of God went through a paradigmatic change from a dominant figure to a crawling one. Cho's revelatory encounter of God among the *minjung* of the *minjung* was historically preceded by an incident sometime in the 1870s. Haewol, who was a leader of Eastern Learning, a Korean *minjung* religion, once visited the home of one of his members on a hot summer day. Discovering the member's daughter-in-law weaving, Haewol asked him, "Is your daughter-in-law weaving or is God weaving?" In the patriarchal society of old Korea, the woman, and especially the woman as daughter-in-law, was the most oppressed one in the Confucian family system. She had to wake up at dawn and work until evening in the field, come home to prepare dinner and care for children, weave till midnight, and then become sexual prey for her husband in bed. To name such a woman as a weaving God was quite revolutionary in Korean society in the 1870s. Kim Ji-ha reinterprets this incident in the contemporary Korean context as the following.

> The fact that a woman laborer, who is treated contemptuously as the bottom of this world, does textile work in the severest working condition means that the most precious God does textile work despite of all kinds of suffering. Realize that the woman laborer alienated and suffering in all kinds of contempt, oppression and exploitation is a living and working God here and now, therefore serve that God.[2]

Cho entered Dong-il Textile Company in 1966 and worked there for six months as a laborer. It was the beginning of her eighteen-year commitment to the urban industrial mission for women laborers. The 1960s and 1970s in Korea was the period of rapid economic development driven by the powerful autocratic leadership of the late president Park. South Korean economic growth was the outcome of the unique situation of Korea as a divided nation. The fundamental contradiction in contemporary Korean social, political, economic, and cultural arenas is derived from the tragic division of Korea by the Allied superpowers (the United States and the USSR) after the Japanese surrender in World War II. The political and economic system of South Korea could not help but emerge with a pro-American indigenous leadership supported by the conservative, anti-communist sector of the society. Both the threat from the North and the U.S. military occupation and presence in South Korea allowed an increased emphasis on national security and anticommunism. The Park regime, which seized power through a military coup in 1961, effectively used ideological and cultural conservatism to strengthen its power in an authoritarian-bureaucratic state. Park's educational and cultural policy emphasized the Confucian-based ideology of filial piety and loyalty, granting official awards to self-sacrificing women, faithful daughters-in-law, and virtuous wives. Nurturing moral values and social norms that foster a harmonious community, Korean Confucian culture reinforces the conception of a strong, bureaucratic state capable of depressing any conflicts of interest. According to Lee Hyo-jae, "The creation of such a (Confucian) cultural milieu justified the social conditions under which the state mobilized women as a cheap labor force, which sacrificed itself for national industrialization."[3] Especially in the 1960s and the early 1970s, labor-intensive light industries, based on an abundant low-wage labor force, particularly young single women, greatly contributed to rapid economic growth through exports. Women workers, most of whom came from rural areas, suffered not only from low wages, but from bad working conditions and no unionization. Most of them were young single women who had to help with their family's living expenses and the education of their brothers.

The traditional female labor of spinning and weaving has a five-thousand-year-old history of producing hemp, fur, cotton, and silk. In Korea there had been looms with which women weaved the textures of cotton cloth, ramie cloth, silk, and hemp cloth. The feudal way of producing with looms is called *kilsam. Kilsam* is a traditional manufacturing process of weaving the texture of cotton cloth, ramie cloth, silk, and hemp cloth out of cotton, ramie, cocoons, and hemp. In the old days of a self-sufficient economy, *kilsam,* along with farming, was the basis of the agricultural family economy. *Kilsam* was one of women's main tasks at home. Here is a loom song expressing *han* and the humor of weaving women in the old times.

> *Chilkong-chalgong* weaving on a loom in front of front door,
> an obituary notice of my dad's death came in.
> Father-in-law, father-in-law, shall I go or not?
> Finish weaving the hemp cloth before you go.
> *Chilkong-chalgong* weaving on a loom in front of back door,
> an obituary notice of my mom's death came in.
> Mother-in-law, mother-in-law, shall I go or not?
> Finish weaving the hemp cloth before you go.
> finish weaving the hemp cloth before you go.
>
> After finishing weaving, I climbed over a hill;
> the cry of my brother's wife shook all village.
> Brother's wife, brother's wife, open the door, open the door;
> what kind of daughter are you? what kind of daughter are you?
> (a loom-song in the province of Boryung)[4]

A Korean woman in the feudal era, especially a daughter-in-law, was a slave without a slave document. The above loom-song sufficiently reveals the sorrow of a daughter-in-law's life in her husband's house and her alienated labor of weaving. Since the Industrial Revolution new machines were invented and the technology of spinning and weaving was greatly improved. The textile industry became a key industry. Since the 1930s many synthetic fibers have been invented and the textile industry continued to grow. It was first introduced to Korea during Japanese rule, but its real growth took place in the 1960s when the Korean government supported it as a key national industry for export. Weaving was traditionally the daughter-in-law's work, but since the 1960s modern textile work in Korea became the work of young woman laborers. The latter as well as the former was an alienated labor. Thus weaving is the symbol of women's suffering. Therefore, one has to use the metaphor of weaving critically. The female labor of weaving or spinning was also recognized by Jesus as hard and toilsome work:

> And why do you worry about clothes? See how the lilies of the field grow. They do not labor or spin. Yet I tell you that not even Solomon in all his splendor was dressed like one of these. If that is how God clothes the grass of the field, which is here today and tomorrow is thrown into the fire, will he not much more clothe you. O you of little faith (Matthew 6:28-30)?

The many clothes "Made in Korea" that are sold in K-mart and Walmart in the United States are the products of the cheap labor and toilsome spinning of young Korean female weavers. What was Jesus' alternative for worrying about the inhuman process of making and wearing clothes? Jesus said, "So do not worry, saying, 'What shall we wear?' . . . But seek first his Kingdom and his righteousness." (Matthew 6:31, 33) Here Jesus indicates there could be two kinds of weaving. One is for the world of unrighteousness and domination, and the other is for the kingdom of God and divine righteousness.

Recently the metaphor of weaving has been widely used by progressive theologians concerned about eco-feminism. Emphasizing the positive aspect of it, most of them tend to ignore the negative side of it. Of course, the beautiful metaphor of weaving is well suited to imagining human participation in the creating, reconciling, and redeeming work of the triune God. Yet if one loses sight of the actual physical work of weaving done by poor Third World women, such a metaphor could become superficial and romanticized. Therefore, before one uses such a metaphor, first think of your own clothes. Who wove them, how were they woven, and in what working conditions? And what is your own weaving for the kingdom of God in your concrete situation?

Cho Wha-soon's six-month experience of labor in Dong-il Textile Company was painful and enlightening at the same time. Cho was thirty-four years old and quite a bit older than most of the Dong-il factory workers. She had to begin her work not in front of spinning and weaving machinery but in a factory kitchen. Since she was a newcomer and an unskilled older worker, she was insulted and humiliated by a forewoman. Feeling shame and anger, Cho bursted into tears. This was her self-transforming experience. She said, "I was crying while I'm working that day. They might think I was crying because I was mistreated. But it was the tears of repentance."[5] Through her experience of shame and humiliation, she went down to the bottom of Korean society at the time. Through her repentance of her pride as an educated clergywoman, she got rid of her patronizing attitude toward other factory workers. Through giving up her false hope of imposing the Gospel on the laborers, she could start an authentic witness to the kingdom of God. Yes, through being with the suffering weavers of our time, she could lead them to weave for the kingdom of God in the sense that they learned to form and transform their own life story. Reflecting on Cho's life story, one can realize that her life is like a quilt done with many persons. Though unskilled in textile work, Cho was an excellent weaver in enabling her co-workers to weave the texture of their own lives. She was the author and co-author of her life, together with the Dong-il Textile women workers. Re-writing her own life as a textile worker, she lured the textile workers to re-write the texts of their lives. Her mission work, therefore, can be called her "practice of narrativity,"[6] i.e., her ongoing activity of both writing her life and helping women workers write their lives.

The Dong-il Textile Company had thirteen hundred members among whom more than one thousand were women. However, all the local committee chairpersons of the labor union in the company were men. The union was pro-government and was not concerned about the suffering of the majority, who were women workers. Instead, the male-dominated union negotiated with the company for the union leaders' own benefit. Therefore, Cho and her fellow women workers, after some labor education and a practice election to overcome the workers' passivity and resignation, decided to turn the union upside down and to form a new union representing women's voices by electing delegates. At last, in 1972, the election of union leaders at Dong-il Textile Company did not change just the Dong-il Textile union, it also changed the whole history of labor unions in Korea. It was the first election of a woman chairperson, Chu Kil-ja. Chu Kil-ja passed out because she was so anxious that she had taken a sedative, but had taken too much. This whole process reminds us again of the women weaving or quilting together their own life textures. Indeed, Cho was a master quilter, and the rest of women workers also became her fellow quilters. Quilting is a communal process of stitching together in new ways scraps of materials that have been used elsewhere. Cho's and her fellow quilters' emancipatory praxis is analogous to such painful yet joyful stitching together in life-giving ways scraps of broken lives. Indeed, stitching in quilting is preceded by discovering and gathering scraps, like opening up wounds in a surgical operation.

After their initial victory, Cho and her fellow quilters went through unbearable suffering just as the Israelites wandered in the wilderness after the Exodus. Just as the Pharaoh did not allow the Israelites to leave Egypt, the Park regime persecuted Cho and the workers. In 1975 a new chairperson took office--again, a woman, Lee Young-sook. But the continuation of an all-women executive committee in the union was viewed as a threat, not only by the company but by the government as well. The police arrested chairperson Lee by setting up a false incident, and the women workers entered into a fast and sit-in. The sit-in, a legal protest, continued for three days. On the second day the company locked all the restrooms and shut off the water and electricity. On the third day the workers were lying exhausted, hot, and hungry. Cho depicted the agonizing scene of their arrest.

Evening came. A bus brought riot police, armed with clubs. They surrounded the workers and began forcibly arresting them. Then an astonishing thing happened: the women workers took off their clothes to protest the arrests. In the hot summer heat of forty degrees centigrade, the workers were mostly wearing only bras under their work clothes; so when they removed these they were half-naked. In that state they sang as loudly as they could, thinking that not even the worst policeman would lay his hands on a naked woman's body. But the police brutally arrested them, beating them with clubs, and the helpless women ran and fell, screaming and bleeding. A few women, in a last desperate act to defend the union, even took off their underpants, but the police seized them just the same and threw them into the bus. Some were beaten and dragged to the bus by their hair. Some women lay in front of the wheels of the bus to try to stop it from taking the workers.[7]

It was literally a nude demonstration! Was it such a shame on them in a Confucian patriarchal context like Korea? Who had to be ashamed of such an incident, the workers or the puppets of an inhuman dictatorship? The women workers toiled day and night to produce the textiles, yet they could not find anything to wear in the end. Yes, what a shame on all Koreans proud of rapid economic growth! Nevertheless, their nakedness and vulnerability was paradoxically the highest point of their emancipatory quilting praxis. The sufferer in Psalm 22 shouts:

> Dogs have surrounded me;
> a band of evil men has encircled me,
> they have pierced my hands and my feet.
> I can count all my bones;
> people stare and gloat over me.
> They divide my garments among them
> and cast lots for my clothing (Psalm 22: 16-18).

The Gospels identify Jesus on the cross with the nude sufferer and protester in the above Psalm. An authentic contemporary practice of narrativity, which aims at weaving for the kingdom of God, has to be led by the Spirit of God in order to incorporate the emancipatory praxis of the nude women demonstrators in partnership with Jesus the Liberator. They were no longer passive miserable women. "Let the weak be strong" is the essence of Cho's rhetoric of liberation that turned the women workers into assertive and self-confident women.

2. Rhetoric of Liberation

The goal of Cho's rhetoric of liberation was "persuasion to emancipatory praxis." The following text of a prayer illumines the quintessence of her rhetoric of liberation.

> There are many struggles around us. Not just struggle, but unjust struggle; not legitimate struggle, but coward struggle; the strong's struggle to exploit the weak; the rich's struggle to mistreat the poor; the powerful's struggle to abuse the *minjung;* man's struggle to oppress woman; the adult's struggle to deceive the young. . . . God of justice who grants power to the weak!. . . . Look into Thy little lambs who were kicked out of their jobs after dung was thrown on them because they wanted a just labor union. As Thou told us, if they belong to the world, they may be loved by the world. Since they are chosen by Thee, the world hate them. However strong the power of this world, how can it stand the power of the heaven? Let those who abuse power and fail to know themselves repent, and let us forgive them. I do believe that the young women factory workers can keep on fighting for justice and will taste the joy of victory in the end as long as, dear Father, Thou protect them under Thy wings. "The day of Yahweh's coming will not be bright, it will rather be dark and there will be no light." The more earnestly these words were felt in the hearts of the oppressed, the sooner the "rooster crying" dawn will be opened like a flash of light.[8]

The rhetorical argument of this prayer consists of three steps, i.e., "to name what is going on, to reveal distortion and corruption, to imagine possibilities out of present reality."[9] Every step is charged with strong pathos as well as a call for action. Just as John Wesley's hermeneutic of sanctification consists of three parts, namely, conviction of sin and repentance, the forgiving grace of Christ and justification, sanctification and Christian perfection, so Cho's rhetoric of liberation consists of three parts: indignation and protest against injustice, liberation from unjust law, and the righteousness of God, envisioning reconciliation, reunification, and interliving to overcome division, conflict, and interkilling. The common aspect of both the hermeneutic of sanctification and the rhetoric of liberation is Spirit-centered divine-human participation.

Cho calls the first step indignation. When women take off their clothes to protest arrest and dung-soaked rags are pushed into their mouths to stop them from decrying injustice, we can only be overwhelmed with indignation. The Dong-il Textile Company fired 124 women workers in 1978. Furthermore, they were on the blacklist and could not be hired by any other companies in Korea. They were forced to go out on the street in the middle of winter. It was a death and a killing. They had nothing to lose. What's going on? Cho names it "not just struggle, but unjust struggle." Indignation is the suffering women's way of knowing the structural evil in our society. This knowledge does not come from any academic study, it only comes out of life experience. The women realize that their keeping silent in the midst of injustice and social evil is a sin. Out of indignation they ask, "Why do I have to live with all this nonsense? Do my daughters have to live the same life as I have lived? Is this kind of life normal and right?"[10] Then, and only then, can a just, not an unjust, struggle for survival and dignity begin, because withdrawal from the battlefield means giving up their bodies to poverty and discrimination.

The woman laborers called Cho "Cho Inspiration." Whenever Cho heard moving stories in their struggle against injustice, Cho kept saying "Wonderful! Wonderful!" Thus the laborers nicknamed her Cho Inspiration, not because she was sensitive by nature but because she was open to the inspiration of the Spirit present and working in the laborers. Such an inspiring experience is different from the experience provided by the charismatic leaders of the Korean church whose leadership is one-way and patriarchal. The charismatic leaders, as the personified symbols of Christian faith, inspire the congregation through their one-way communication of caring and loving. The congregation cannot be differentiated from the charismatic leaders. It depends utterly on the external authority of the leaders. Cho's leadership differed from the charismatic leadership. She not only recognized the value and power of each and every woman worker but appreciated it and was inspired by it. In other words, the woman laborers were differentiated from Cho, yet they still formed a community together. Cho's leadership was interactive and accepting. In fact Cho was constantly accused of being a "red" or a procommunist by the government and the conservative leaders of the Korean church because she agitated the ignorant laborers. Her response to her critics was that they underestimated the laborers. One result of the undemocratic education of patriarchal Korean society was to see the laborers as mere passive beings who could not voluntarily act because they are not educated. According to Cho, "the law of forbidding the intervention of the third party," one of the bad labor laws, was caused by the sheer ignorance of the political and economic leaders who did not realize the progressive character of the laborers as the subjects of history. By means of the epistemology of indignation, the laborers can achieve a third-person perspective from which they can objectively and critically view their problems in relation to the social

113

structure, unlike most middle-class citizens who can hardly break their conventional value systems.

The second step in Cho's rhetoric of liberation is "breaking the unjust law." Since Cho had struggled to protest against the economic policy and dictatorship of the Korean government which had taken sides with the capitalists, she had to violate the unjust law of the state and had gone to prison four times. Cho broke a false image of the shy and weak woman and embodied a new image of the assertive and wise woman. Her first imprisonment in 1974 was caused by her preaching on "Search for the Kingdom and for Righteousness." In her sermon, Cho criticized the government because it arrested many human rights leaders, ministers, and university students who violated the Emergency Decree. In the name of the so-called Korean democracy, the Park regime had promulgated the Korean hypocrisy involved in the Yushin Constitution that guaranteed Park's life-long dictatorship. Cho was again imprisoned in 1978 after she gave a fiery speech at a public meeting about the fight of the Dong-il Textile workers. Cho was charged with violation of Presidential Emergency Decree No. 9 and violation of the Law on Meeting and Demonstrations. Before she began her summary statement at the court, she prayed quietly, "Dear Lord, help me not to speak with my head but to let the Holy Spirit lead me to say what you want me to say."[11] The courage to break rules cannot be born unless one is determined to die (Esther 4:15-16). Where does the courage to not fear even death come from? Cho claims that such courage is possible not by thinking with the head but by being led by the Holy Spirit. This is the living witness of a person who took up her cross in the context of suffering under the guidance of the Holy Spirit. Such a witness is totally different from the egotistic witness of material blessing and physical healing by the Holy Spirit. Only when one goes beyond the boundary of selfish security and happiness in order to be in communion with suffering neighbors, can one realize the profound will of God governing history. This is a life led not by the head but by the Holy Spirit. It is not merely the witness of an individual anointed by the Holy Spirit but the prophecy of one who takes side with the suffering people, a prophecy inspired by the Spirit of God who is leading history. Cho describes what she said and how she acted in the court when she was allowed by the judge to speak:

> I continued my story in a somewhat excited state. "In Luke's Gospel, some people came to Jesus and warned, 'Herod is trying to kill you! Please hurry and escape!' But instead of escaping, Jesus told them, 'Go and tell the fox

that today and tomorrow, I will chase Satan away and heal the sick, then the third day I will finish my work. Today, tomorrow and the day after, I have to go my way. Could a prophet die anywhere else but in Jerusalem?' As a disciple of Jesus, I am doing this work with the same mind as Jesus." I turned to the courtroom audience and shouted, "Even though a crowd of devils like Herod tries to kill me, I will fight against them without fear of death. My friends the workers are the same. We will fight the devils of this land, not fearing death. The *han* of all the oppressed, poor, and marginalized will turn into the sword--the dagger--of God's judgment and stab deep into the hearts of the devils. Our chief, Jesus, is leading us. We will surely have victory. Hurrah for the workers of this land! Hurrah for God!" The tears ran down my face. The judge said something to try to stop me, but none of his words were audible to me. When I finished speaking, all those in attendance stood and clapped warmly. They were all weeping.[12]

Cho's prophecy was fulfilled. Just a few months later, president Park was assassinated by one of his own men. President Chun and President Loh, who were Park's successors and imitated Park's authoritarian rule, have also been judged by God and imprisoned. History has eloquently shown that Cho's and her friends" breaking the rules was right. Through breaking the unjust law, Cho did not merely challenge the dictatorship but she liberated herself and many other women from the age-old Confucian patriarchy in family, church, and society. Cho was not a fighter by birth. She was made a fighter by her commitment to the Urban Industrial Mission. She used to be depicted as if she were an iron, aggressive, and masculine agitator. The prosecutor accused her of agitating class struggle. Cho's famous last statement in the court also seems to confirm Cho's bellicose nature. However, if one sees her from the *han*-ridden perspective of all the oppressed, poor, and marginalized, especially the women workers, her radical actions reveal the distortion and corruption of humanity and faith in both Koreanized democracy and patriarchal Christianity. Such revealing of the truth by violating evil laws demands self-denial and self-sacrifice. The basis of Cho's rhetorical argument is the law of God by which one challenges the unjust law of the state. The law of God for Cho is not a transcendental norm but a material norm concretely affecting present reality. Cho also calls it the promise of God that God makes the weak strong (2 Corinthians 12:10). Therefore, this norm does not sanction the status quo of the present patriarchal reality in both church and society. Instead it supports emancipatory praxis. It is messianic and future-oriented while it is transformative and realistic.

The third step of Cho's rhetoric of liberation is to envision the messianic life of interliving by embracing the connectedness of the whole creation.

Between Cho's last speech in the court in 1978 and her recent preaching on World Day of Prayer in 1997, there has been a great deal of change and maturation in her rhetoric of liberation.[13] Twenty years ago she alluded to her struggle as a battle with devils outside of herself and her comrades. Reflecting her own struggle against structural evil, Cho confessed in a recent sermon that she tried to eliminate evil completely. However, the more furiously she and her comrades fought against the evil out there, the more severely their personhood was wounded. She became to realize that she was exposed to the danger and temptation of self-righteousness and inflexibility within herself. In other words, the evil did not simply exist outside her as an external substance, but remains inside herself. Whenever one fights against evil, one is tempted to take pride in one's critical consciousness and moral integrity. This can lead to a spiritual awakening of the deeper self, i.e., the discovery of the dynamics of the unconscious drive for domination. Cho preached in her sermon not to eliminate the evil inside as well as outside but to coexist with it in the sense that the good is strengthened through embracing the evil, that is, the good overcomes the evil by the good. This change in her rhetoric, however, should not be misinterpreted either as a compromise with evil or as the weakening and softening of her radicality.

The devils Cho tried to kill twenty years ago are not dead! Who are the devils anyway? In her ministry at Dokjokdo, Cho exorcised the devil from a mad person. The devil was the *han*-ridden spirit residing in the deep unconscious level of poor people in a Shamanistic agricultural context. Cho tried hard to name and exorcise the devil by using the system of Christian symbols. It was a spiritual-cultural struggle between the premodern Shamanistic life-world and the modern Western Christian life-world. When the devil was identified with a white-haired old man from a Shaman's house, Cho forced the possessed person to repeat the name of the triune God so that the old man could get away from the household of the mad man.[14] There was repressed guilt on the side of Cho, the exorcist, and bypassed shame on the side of the 'old man" in the possessed.

This antagonism between two different spiritual and cultural world-views did not disappear in Cho's struggle against the devils in the industrialized divided Korea. It is significant to note that Cho still continued to use Shamanistic, premodern language like "the devil." Of course, the meaning of devil was demythologized by the concept of structural evil in a modern capitalist Korean society. Here the conventional dogmatic form of Christianity, which was pro-dictatorship and patriarchal, and Cho's postconventional critical form of Christian faith were in mutual conflict.

The tragic aspect of her heroic struggle was her own victimization in the process of interkilling between the devils and the devils' antagonist. When it comes to a devil such as anticommunism, omnipresent in every arena of South Korean culture, politics, education, and religion, it is not a matter of getting rid of the devil but of healing the Korean psyche through integrating its other side. In other words, it is not a matter of killing the devil but of taming it.

Cho's re-entry into the ministry of Dalwol Methodist Church in a small village in 1983 gave her a great opportunity to grow spiritually. It was not like her first ministry in Dokjokdo nor like her Urban Industrial Mission. Yet it integrated both the repressed and bypassed elements from the former and the critical and liberative praxis from the latter. Cho's ministry and life after 1983 typifies the traits of rebuilding 'public church'. Public church is an ideal community of faith "that can hold together both deep Christian commitment and a principled openness and effective contribution to the common good in a pluralistic and increasingly crowded world."[15] The total population of the village was about five hundred. Cho prayed hard and diligently made home visitations in order to overcome the Dalwol congregation's suspicion of the new human rights pastor. She wholeheartedly loved them regardless of their economic and social status or their educational backgrounds. She tried her best to have everybody involved in the sacraments and worship. Cho developed three major programs for the village: the Farmers' Credit Union, a Community Newsletter, and a nursery and kindergarten. Gradually Cho led the Dalwol congregation into a new experience of becoming involved in issues of farmers' rights. The villagers who had been intimidated by the government authorities for a long time learned about their own citizens' rights in a concrete context. One of the Dalwol congregation who was not happy with the appointment of Cho in the beginning was completely changed later and confessed: "To encounter Rev. Cho means to go beyond myself. It's to transcend my family, to give up peace and security. It's not to compromise with reality, but to live a prophetic life."

The significant clue to the third step of Cho's rhetoric of liberation comes from her experience of the healing of repressed guilt and by-passed shame.[16] One day when Cho was coming back from home visitation, she saw a few old men sitting at the corner of a village store and drinking *soju*, a popular Korean alcohol. They looked so pure and honest to her. She was deeply touched and had compassion on them. She said to them, "Dear grandpa, I want to buy *soju* for you." The non-Christian old men were surprised by the village pastor's unconventional kindness and rather worried about her reputation if the elders of

Dalwol Church heard about the incident. After the incident, Dalwol Church served food and drink (including *soju,* of course) to all the villagers on every Thanksgiving Sunday. Why did Cho encounter the face of God in the dark wrinkled old farmers' faces which looked so honest, pure, and mild? The image of an old man was the image of patriarchy in her past. It is no wonder that Cho drove out an 'old man' from the possessed person in Dokjokdo. At the time, the image of an old man was devilish. But later it was changed into the face of God who suffered. This shows Cho's reconciliation with her deeper self, i.e., her Shamanistic and *minjung* roots. It also shows that she became mature enough not to eliminate the devils of anticommunism or of patriarchy, but to tame them to surrender to the justice of God which is realized not through interkilling but through interliving. When Cho preached her sermon on "Women Making Peace," she radiated peace, composure, and deliberation and looked proud, victorious, and self-aware.

> God uses the weak to make the strong ashamed. God wants to realize through us women peace, truth, love and justice on this earth. God expects us women to prepare the feast day to embrace our beloved ones and to share around the table and to dance in the Spirit.[17]

---

1) For the difference between communicative competence and linguistic competence, see Juergen Habermas, tr. by Thomas McCarthy, *Communication and the Evolution of Society* (Beacon Press, 1979), xviii.

2) Kim Ji-ha, *Rice* (Bundo Publishing House, 1993), 53.

3) Lee Hyo-jae, "The Social Background of Cho Wha-soon's Ministry," in Cho Wha-soon, *Let the Weak be Strong* (Meyer Stone Books, 1988), 147.

4) "A loom-song from the province of Boyrung," *Contemporary Korean Literature 3* (Kemongsa Publishing Co., 1995), 222-223.

5) The Study Group of the Association of Korean Woman Theologians, *A Flame of Love in the Midst of Suffering* (Christian Literature Society of Korea, 1992). 74.

6) Rebecca S. Chopp, *Saving Work* (Westminister John Knox Press, 1995), 34.

7) Cho Wha-soon, *op. cit.,* 65.

8) *A Flame of Love in the midst of Suffering,* 134-135.

9) Chopp, *op. cit.,* 92.

10) The Publication Committee of the Festschrift for the Rev. Cho Wha-soon, *A Life inspired by Suffering and Hope* (The Saenoori Newspaper, 1994), 279.

11) Cho Wha-soon, *op. cit.,* 99.

12) *Ibid.,* 99-100.

13) Cf. Cho Wha-soon's unpublished sermon "Little Seeds" preached on the 1997 World Day of Prayer.

14) Cf. My interview with Rev. Cho Wha-soon (April 3, 1997).

15) James W. Fowler, *Weaving the New Creation* (Cokesbury, 1991), xiv.

16) Cf. My interview with Rev. Cho.

17) *A Flame of Love in the Midst of Suffering*, 308.

CHAPTER 9

The Trinitarian Structure of Theology of the Spirit

1. The Weak Change Civilization *(Kungul hoe mun myung)*

G OD CHOSE THE WEAK things of the world to shame the strong (1 Cor. 1:27).

On July 1, 1997 the last great world-historical event in the twentieth century happened. The return (not handover) of Hong Kong from the British Empire to the People's Republic of China symbolized the long-delayed ending of "the Western domination of the East". In the return ceremony the Asian Youth Orchestra performed the "Symphony 1997 Heaven, Earth, Human Being" for the first time. Yes, for the first time the 1.2 billion people of China entered a new era opening up a new heaven and a new earth. The harmony of heaven, earth, and human being is the primal vision of East Asian civilization. This vision is closely connected with the cosmological-circular theory of fortune which originated from the *I-Ching* (the Book of Change). Among the divination signs in the *I-Ching*, hexagram 12 (P'i), which means stagnation, consists of the pure *yang*-heaven above and the pure *yin*-earth below, while hexagram 11 (Tai), which means peace, consists of the pure *yin*-earth above and the pure *yang*-heaven below. Prince Charles did not apologize for British colonial rule in Hong Kong. Instead he mentioned the economic achievement and democratization of Hong Kong under British rule. Prime minister Jang of China claimed that China would experiment with "one nation, two systems" for the next 50 years. The prime minister declared that the return of Hong Kong means world peace and the victory of justice. On the day after the Union Jack went down and the Five Star went up, there was a demonstration for peace in Hong Kong. Hundreds of thousands of people who remembered the Tienanmen massacre on June 4, 1989, participated in the demonstration. Whether the return of Hong Kong means the inversion of heaven and earth so that a new heaven and a new earth will be opened up remains to be seen in the future history of China.

When China lost her sovereignty after the Opium War in the 1840s, the political order of Asia was in fundamental transition. Since the delusion of China as the center of the world was broken, East Asia fell victim to Western and Japanese colonialism. Japan became a colonial power after she went through the Meiji Restoration aimed at "Out of Asia, Into Europe." Korea faced a double crisis: the corrupt government oppressed the *minjung* on the one hand and the colonial powers threatened the Korean *minjung* on the other hand. The messianic expectation of the groaning Korean *minjung* for a new heaven and a new earth brought about the *minjung*-religious movement and resulted in a peasant uprising which was brutally subdued by the feudalistic power aided by Japanese colonialism. The Donghak (Eastern Learning) Peasant War in 1894 was the peak of the *minjung*-messianic movement in nineteenth century Korea. The Donghak movement, which began in the 1860s was led by indigenous spiritual leaders such as Suun and Haewol who envisioned "opening-up of the latter heaven". They used the symbol *Kung Kung ul ul* which is related to the *yin-yang* symbol. *Kung* literally means bow and bird. Both signify flying. The shape of both symbols also reminds us of the *yin-yang* movement. When the double *kungul* are matched together, they become *yak* which means the weak. The era of the latter heaven will be the era in which the weak change civilization.

There is a very interesting colloquial expression in Korean. It is *kungkung-I-sok* which refers to an inscrutable personality. The facade of a person could be very different from his or her *kungkung-I-sock*. *Kungkung* is also the sound of unbearable pain. The genius of Donghak is derived from the amazing conjunction of the highly metaphysical symbol Kung Kung and the moans and groans of the suffering *minjung*. *Kungkung* refers to the messianic horizon of the Korean *minjung* yearning for salvation. Suun, the pioneer of Donghak, wrote a hymn on *kungkung*:

> Even the heart of a corrupt official beats with *kungkung*,
> the heart of a rich old man beats with *kungkung*,
> the heart of a wandering beggar beats with *kungkung*.
> Those drifting people look for a *kungkung* village,
> or they hide themselves in high mountains,
> or they join Western Learning (Roman Catholicism).
> And each and every one of them claims
> "I am right, you are wrong."

Every hour and every minute they say,
"We are right, you are wrong."[1]

One can say that Korean *minjung* culture is *kungkung* culture. The phonetic representation of the famous Korean rhythm *semachi* is *dung-dung-duk-kung-duk*. *Kung* is the sound of the left side of *jangu*, the famous Korean two-sided drum, *duk* is the sound of the right side and *dung* is the sound of both sides. *Kung* is the sound of earth corresponding with *duk* the sound of heaven. Without the groans and moans of earth, the sound of heaven hardens: *duk* becomes *tak*. When the sounds of both earth and heaven are in harmony, one can dance *dung-sil, dung-sil* (cheerfully). This typical Korean three-beat rhythm *dung-duk-kung* is connected with typical Korean shoulder dancing. The mysterious pulse from the shoulder is caused by the fuzzy beat between the right side of the drum and the left side of drum, or between heaven-*yang* and earth-*yin*. When one plays *jangu*, one must concentrate on 'triunity' in one's body: jaws, belly, and knees which are related to heaven, human beings, and earth respectively. The drummer breathes according to the circle of life which operates in microcosm as well as in macrocosm. Then the mysterious fuzzy beat moves one to feel a pulse from the shoulder. *Dung-dung-duk-kung-duk, dung-dung-duk-kung-duk, ...* This beat goes on and on. Dancing follows naturally and spontaneously. Arms gracefully move in front of the dancer and behind the dancer as if one drew a *yin-yang* shape while heels move slightly up and down. The best dancing is the spirited dancing which freely rides on the fuzzy beat between *yin* and *yang*. Such dancing moves as if it released long suppressed life energy from inside to outside and received life-giving power from outside to inside. One's *han (kungkung* ache) inside is relieved and one feels cool because one is no longer choked by resentment and *han*. One cannot dance unless one gets spirited or the Spirit grasps one. Only then can one confess, "You turned my wailing into dancing" (Psalms 30:11).

Kim Ji-ha, the Korean poet and thinker, asserts that *kungkung* is the archetype of a new chaos or a new civilization.[2] The rational, moral principle of the old civilization, *logos* or *li*, refers to the explicit order of the cosmos. *Kungkung* can be understood as the symbol of Great *ch'i* (   ) which is the life energy or the implicit order of chaos. A new civilization does not exclude modern Western scientific civilization. Instead, a new civilization combines it with the life-centered, spiritual tradition of the East. *Kungkung* will change civilization. *Kungkung* does not come from Confucianist patriarchalism, which had been predominant in neo-Confucian orthodoxy, but from *minjung* Shamanistic traditions, which had

122

provided fertile soil for the indigenization of the Gospel. In one of the Donghak sects, the *kungkung* symbol became an indigenous symbol for the cross. If Kung and the flip side of Kung are combined, it becomes the shape of cross. The Donghak sectarians called it a cross as well as the tree of life. When the Gospel of Jesus Christ was proclaimed in Korea in the 1880s, there must have been a great economy (*oikonomia*) of the triune God. According to St. Paul, the *oikonomia* of the triune God is revealed in the partnership of Christians with the crucified God in the Spirit.

> When I came to you, brothers, I did not come with eloquence or superior wisdom as I proclaimed to you the testimony about God. For I resolved to know nothing while I was with you except Jesus Christ and him crucified. I came to you in weakness and fear, and with much trembling. My message and my preaching were not with wise and persuasive words, but with a demonstration of the Spirit's power, so that your faith might not rest on men's wisdom, but on God's power (1 Corinthians 2:1-5).

Protestant mission work in Korea was oriented toward the lower-class such as the outcast class of butchers. A large number of them were converted to the Christian faith. After the Donghak Peasant War, the countryside was wide open for evangelism. Many people who participated in the Donghak movement became Christians. The miraculous growth of the Korean church was the product of an evangelism not of "wise and persuasive words" but of "a demonstration of the Spirit's power." The beginning of the Great Revival of the Korean church in 1907 was penetrated by Korean Christians' passionate commitment to partnership with the God who was crucified and still works in the Spirit. The *minjung* Christians of the early Korean church remind us of the Corinthian Christians, not many of whom were wise, influential, and of noble birth. The messianic expectations of the Donghak movement for the opening up of a new era, in which *kungkung,* or the weak, change civilization, were fulfilled in the proclamation of the Gospel that "God chose the weak things of the world to shame the strong" (1 Corinthians 1:27).

The problem of the community in Corinth was caused by pneumatics whose proto-Gnostic enthusiasm for exaltation Christology made them curse the historical Jesus. They considered themselves *christoi* (christs) who annihilated the *sarx* (flesh). The formula of their Christology is best summed up in the creed: Christ died and rose again. This seems to be orthodox. However, it can be interpreted to mean that death is nullified and that faith now has to focus solely on the exalted Christ. For pneumatics, faith became the movement of spiritual ascent along with the Redeemer. Such faith resulted in the detachment of believers from the world. Through ecstatic experiences of the Spirit, pneumatics were caught up out of the world into heaven. This Gnostic theology of the Spirit avoids the theology of the cross which keeps the historic character of faith alive.

In the history of the Holy Spirit movement of the Korean church there has always been an unresolved problem of the theology of the Spirit in opposition to the theology of the cross.

The majority of the Western missionaries who came to Korea preached a faith based on pietism and evangelism, separating Korean believers from social involvement. For instance, when Korea lost her national sovereignty in 1905, prophetic Korean Christians took the lead in the anti-Japan struggles. Missionaries endeavored to thwart such prophetic participation. They were suspected of leading a revival movement in 1907 in an attempt to steer the Korean church toward depoliticizing Korean Christians. Though the United States was not a colonial power in Korea, North American missionaries certainly had a colonialistic missiology which was coopted by the national interests of the United States. W. N. Blair represented such a colonialistic missiology:

> We felt . . . that embittered souls needed to have their thoughts taken away from the national situation to their own personal relation with the Master.[3]

The reactionary movement of spiritual ascent along with the Master hypnotized many Korean Christians to flee the suffering and victory of the cross. In the dear name of a personal relation with the sweet Master, the faith of Korean Christians was 'bleached' by the 'wise and persuasive words' of the White missionaries. Of course the cheap Gospel sold well. Yet it suffocated costly discipleship. The 'chlorine' of colonialistic missiology was dumped into the lakes and streams of the history of the Korean church. The fateful internalization of the colonialistic missiology has been apparent in the fundamentalist theology and sectarian ethical views of the majority of Korean Christians. For them, God was confined in time to a sacred Sunday and in space to a transcendental other world. God was believed to rest from the mundane world during the week days and to work busily only on Sunday and in heaven. The spiritual sphere was split from the temporal sphere. Because of such dualism, many Korean Christians began to lose the historic character of their faith and became reluctant to share the sufferings of the *minjung*.

Was there no voice in the wilderness of the modern history of Korea? Fortunately there was one. Unfortunately, however, the voice also came from the wilderness of the Korean church. Ham Suk-hun (1901-1989) was neither a minister nor a theologian, but he was the first person who interpreted the suffering history of the Korean *minjung* from a biblical perspective. Ham was struck by the biblical view of the providence of God in human history. He was a history teacher and a lay Christian, and later he gave up the Christian faith to embrace 'universalizing faith.' His contribution to democracy and human rights twice made him a candidate for the Nobel peace prize. Despite his unorthodox faith, his prophetic life and teaching should not be excluded from the Korean theology of the Spirit. Ham's uniqueness of thought is a creative synthesis of a theory of providence and a *minjung* perspective in the interpretation of Korean history. Ham's basic thesis is that God, the creator and governor of the world, works through God's partners, the *minjung*, in history.

Ham calls *minjung si-al* (seed with an embryo bud). *Al* (embryo bud) in Korean consists of three parts: heaven, human being, and earth. *Si-al* is the self-conscious life in human history as well as in the universe. Heaven and earth have to meet each other and the human being has to labor in order for a *si-al* to grow. As a seed must fall on the ground and die to give fruit, *si-al* must suffer to become the subject of history. Ham considers Korean history a history of suffering. Korea has never invaded other countries. But she has been invaded by China, Manchuria, Mongolia, and Japan. Since 1945 Korea was divided by the United States and the Soviet Union. The Korean War broke out in 1950. Ham's prophetic imagination let him perceive the "trembling hands of God" in the division and war of Korea. God used the military forces of both the United States and the Soviet Union as the trembling hands of God by which *si-al*, the Korean *minjung*, were tested and disciplined.

> The 38th parallel is the line breaking the heart of our nation. Has *si-al* ripened? Or is it mere husk? God split it with God's trembling hands. What are the rifles, machine guns, bombs and airplanes of the military forces of both the United States in South and the Soviet Union in North? Aren't they the trembling hands of God? If *si-al* ripens, it is one. Such oneness makes God delighted. If it is yet to ripen, it is dead husk divided into two.[4]

According to Ham, when the superpowers came into Korea, the Korean *minjung* should have declared that "We are one nation." Tragically, however, the Korean *minjung* were misled by the puppet leaders of both North and South to fight against each other. The Korean War broke out to punish the sin of the Korean nation and to bring forth a new nation for world peace. Ham said, "*Si-al* began to break." When it breaks, it awakens

125

and gives birth to a new life. Ham reads the providence of God in the very process and result of the war. Neither the United States nor the Soviet Union won the war because God used the old ideology and the old power to grow a new life. Ham's metaphorical imagination becomes a prophecy for new age: "So far the flowers of capitalism have blossomed more than enough and have been touched by the frost of communism more than enough. Neither the flowers nor the frost will stay forever. When they will go away, a new *si-al* will ripen."[5] In other words, the flowers of American capitalism and the frost of Russian communism did play their role in history in order to ripen the Korean *minjung* to participate in the *oikonomia* of God. Indeed, it is neither the United States nor the Soviet Union but only God who ripens *si-al*.

> What, after all, is Apollos? And what is Paul? Only servants, through whom you came to believe--as the Lord has assigned to each his task. I planted the seed, Apollos watered it, but God made it grow. So neither he who plants nor he who waters is anything, but only God, who makes things grow. The man who plants and the man who waters have one purpose, and each will be rewarded according to his own labor. For we are God's fellow workers; you are God's field, God's building (1 Corinthians 3:5-9).

Through the *oikonomia* of God, a Paul and an Apollos helped the Korean *si-al* grow. The United States is a Paul, who planted the Christian Gospel, democracy, and capitalism in Korea; the Soviet Union is an Apollos, who cultivated the more authentic character of Korean Christians and the more just structures of Korean politics and economy. Neither a Paul nor an Apollos, but God made the Korean *minjung* grow mature. The Korean *minjung* is God's building (*oikos*) built according to the *oikonomia* of God. The Korean *minjung*, however, have to take off their shoes because they are in God's holy field. Taking off their shoes means stopping wandering and facing the providence of God and one's vocation. The providence of God is revealed in the divine election of the people of God. The election is concrete and universal. The wandering Israelites were elected not because they were a great nation but because God loved them: "The Lord did not set his affection on you and choose you because you were more numerous than other people, for you were the fewest of all peoples. But it was because the Lord loved you" (Deuteronomy 7:7-8). God chose the *si-al* in Korea not because they were a greater nation than the Americans or the Russians but because God wanted to bring out a new civilization through the weak and to shame the strong (1 Corinthians 1:27).

126

Struggling to understand the universal meaning of suffering in life and history, Ham searches the world-historical vocation of the *si-al* in Korea. He viewed the divided Korea as an old harlot whose two hands were pulled hard by China and Russia and whose two legs were pulled by the United States and Japan. For Ham, Korea is like Rodin's famous sculpture, "Woman who was once a prostitute," who, for the last thousand years, has sat beside the highway which runs from the Asian continent and leads to the Pacific Ocean. Because of this fateful geopolitical condition, all the scum of both Eastern and Western civilizations came to Korea. Using Pauline metaphors, Ham said, "We have been made a spectacle to the whole universe, to angels as well as to men" (1 Corinthians 4:9):

> No, we have become the gutter of world-history. But people of the world, thank this gutter. Is it not this gutter that helps you play in the palace of joy? Is it not this gutter that willingly receives and cleans the things you are sick and tired of? Oh, you, the great gutter of world history![6]

To be the gutter of world history does not mean to be low profile. On the contrary, it requires extraordinary gut to become the gutter of world history. The gutter must be connected to the stream of water flowing into the sea. It means that *si-al,* as the gutter of world history, shouldn't be choked by resentment or *han* and should keep its pathway to the infinite sea of God. Therefore, Ham exhorts the Korean *minjung* to bear the cross of world history joyfully. Only the hottest bellows of suffering can purify them from the idolatry of tribal gods, class gods, and ideological gods. His exhortation becomes eloquent preaching without kerygma and the peak of his preaching turns into a hymn of praise devoid of dogma:

> Then, arise, all you who are burdened with suffering. Night fell in Gethsemane and you already crossed the brook in Kidron valley. The end is near. Two thousand years ago the King of suffering said, "Yet not as I will, but as you will," drank the bitter cup of suffering and dared to bear the cross. Let's joyfully take this burden and go down to the sorrowful neck of the last rapids. Let's throw away the rags that made us look beggars. We begged for the rags in the market place of vanity. Let's throw away all we have that have been dear to us. They were the things that we picked up from our rich neighbor's garbage can when we had a vague memory. Let's throw away the doumentdocument which we inherited from our forefathers and have kept in our arms even in sleep. It is the document of the debts of our poor neighbor. Let's forgive those who took away our lands. From now on there is neither your land nor my land. Let's forgive the enemies who killed our father and our grandfather. There is no difference between your nation

127

and my nation, or between your home and my home. Let's throw into this flow the resentment and *han* that was inscribed on our bones with our gnawing teeth when our children were taken away from us. Let's throw into the water the enmity even reaching the tips of hair and the poison tainted in each cell when the beast-like ones captured our virgins and raped our wives in front of us. There is Golgotha beyond this rapids. But it cannot threaten the prince of suffering. Just bear this burden. Bear this cross in love, in faith and in hope to cross the rapids. Then, we can sing a song.

> Closer, closer to my lover
> climbing up to the cross,
> I'm singing all the time;
> closer to my lover
> closer only to my lover
> closer."[7]

2. The Trinity for Interliving

Does the *oikonomia* of God involved in the suffering history of the Korean *minjung* have anything to do with orthodox faith in the triune God? It took almost a half century for Ham Suk-hun's voice in the wilderness to find its echo in the history of the Holy Spirit movement of the Korean church. The Spirit of the Lord was upon Ham when he invited *si-al* to bear the burden of suffering at the peak of his prophecy. Alas! When the Spirit of the Lord was upon the community of faith later, Ham was no longer a Christian. It was not by his religious genius but by faith in the Word of God that he discovered the providence of God in the suffering history of the Korean *minjung*. Both the Israelite prophet Isaiah's insight about the suffering servant and the Christian apostle Paul's kerygma of the crucified Christ were rooted in the life of the faith community. Despite Ham's apparent rejection of Christian dogma and institutions, it was not by his personal imagination but by the inspiration of the Spirit of God that he could make sense out of the suffering history of the Korean *si-al* from a biblical perspective. The Spirit of the Lord grasped Ham to begin to write his famous *Korean History in Biblical Perspective* in the 1930s and the Spirit also inspired the National Council of Churches in Korea to proclaim "Declaration of the Churches of Korea on National Reunification and Peace" in 1988.

> The Spirit of the Lord is upon me,
> because he has anointed me

to preach good news to the poor.
He has sent me
to proclaim release to the captives
and recovering of sight to the blind,
to set at liberty those who are oppressed,
to proclaim the acceptable year of the Lord (Luke 4:18-19).

The Declaration as a whole, and the proclamation of the Jubilee year in particular, represents the repenting and calling of the Korean church. This Jubilee theme is prominent in the Declaration. It is significant to notice that the theme of the upcoming eighth general assembly of the WCC. is also related to the Jubilee theme: "Turn to God, and rejoice in hope." The general secretary of the WCC, Konrad Raiser, suggested celebrating the ecumenical Jubilee when he gave his keynote speech at the 1995 Jubilee consultation of the NCCK. The ecumenical Jubilee movement aims at repentance of the five hundred years of Western colonialism and the one-thousand-year-long division of the church. It also calls for reconciliation and the renewal of covenant to prepare for the third millennium of Christianity. Developing the theme of ecumenical Jubilee in relation to the *oikonomia* of the triune God working in history and the universe is the greatest task of Korean theology of the Spirit.

When the NCCK proclaimed the year 1995 as the Jubilee year for peace and reunification in 1988, no one knew how the providence of God would operate in realizing the Jubilee year. The Declaration describes the significance of the Jubilee year 1995 as follows:

> The Korean churches proclaim 1995, the fiftieth year of our Liberation, as a Jubilee year. This expresses our belief that the God who rules all history has been present within these fifty years of our history, and proclaims our firm resolution to bring about the restoration of the covenanted community of peace in the history of the Korean peninsula today. As we march forward with high aspirations toward this Jubilee year, we should anticipate a revitalizing of our faith in the sovereign God who works within the history of our people, together with a renewing of our commitment to God's mission calling.[8]

Who is the God of the Jubilee year? The sovereign God who rules all history is the God who humbly turns him/herself to the ones who turn to God. The Declaration claims that "Jesus Christ came to this land as the 'Servant of Peace' (Ephesians 2:13-19), to proclaim within division, conflict and oppression God's Kingdom of peace, reconciliation and liberation." The servant of peace is contrasted with the lord of war. The former works for interliving and the latter works for interkilling. The former represents freedom as community and the latter freedom as lordship. God has offered the Jubilee of liberation and reconciliation to us in Jesus Christ which opens up the way of repentance. The Jubilee call is the call for a self-limitation of power in terms of property titles and of domination over slaves. The Jubilee year calls for a conscious self-limitation in the exercise of power in order to restore a sustainable order of human community. God who calls us to the self-limitation of power is the God who him/herself did go through the same process of self-limitation of power in Jesus Christ. The Declaration also affirms that "We believe that the Holy Spirit will reveal to us the eschatological future of history, will make us one, and enable us to become partners in God's mission." The peacemakers are the partners of God in the *oikonomia* of God. Following Jesus Christ, they are led by the Spirit. It is important to notice a trinitarian structure in this *oikonomia* of God.

Not the God of patriarchal monotheism but the God of love, who humbled him/herself and went through the self-limitation of power in Jesus Christ, is affirmed in the Declaration. This affirmation is a prophetic critique of the patriarchal, authoritarian rule of both North and South Korean political powers, regardless of their ideological difference, for the last half century. It is also the confession of the sin of the Korean church which has been coopted by the demonic system of division and has fallen to an ideological idolatry that confuses faith with either communism or with anticommunism.

> The Christians of both North and South have made absolute idols of the ideologies imposed by their respective systems. This is a betrayal of the ultimate sovereignty of God (Exodus 20:3-5), and a sin, for the church must obey the will of God rather than the will of political regimes (Acts 4:19).[9]

The use of the language of divine sovereignty is prominent in the Declaration. However, it is misleading to abuse it to rationalize patriarchal domination in politics and church life. The Declaration's affirmation of Jesus Christ as the Servant of Peace, which needs to be highlighted to warn against an overdose of sovereignty language, does challenge the patriarchal, authoritarian abuse of the North-South Joint Communique of July 4, 1972. After issuing the Joint Communique, in which the three broad principles (independence, peace, and a great national unity) of peace and reunification were articulated, the governments of both North and South instead solidified their authoritarian rule. Therefore, the Declaration suggests adding two other principles to the Joint Communique: one is the maximum protection of human liberty and dignity, and the other is the full democratic participation of all members of society. Furthermore, the Declaration dares to recommend the withdrawal of U.S. troops from Korea if a verifiable state of mutual trust is restored between North and South Korea, and the peace and security of the entire Korean peninsula is guaranteed. Despite its progressive character, the Declaration was criticized in the "Women's Forum of the International Christian Consultation on Justice and Peace in Korea," which was held on April 24-25, 1988, at Inchon, Korea. The Declaration identifies the cause of the division of the Korean peninsula as the world's two superpowers' military and ideological confrontation. But the participants of the Women's Forum saw a deeper cause of division in patriarchalism:

> The division of Korea is a product of the conflict between the U.S. and the U.S.S.R., and a reflection of the fundamental contradiction in the world system. But the more basic cause of the problem is the patriarchal history with its logic of power, of conquering the enemy, of oppression--that is, the logic of the strong dominating the weak. And while patriarchalism has caused the division, in turn the division reinforces the patriarchal structure, in the form of a social, economic and military structure that has sacrificed the human rights of women and suppressed democratic reforms.[10]

Concentrating on the contradictions of the political and ideological division, the Declaration loses sight of the socioeconomic and sexual contradictions, which are caused by the complicity of patriarchalism and capitalism. The result of such complicity is that women's bodies and their labor become the objects of exploitation and the means of obtaining foreign exchange. Under this economic structure, women workers struggling for the right of survival are suppressed by labeling them leftists and procommunists. The presence of U.S. military forces, stationed in Korea since the time of the division, has forced many poor women into prostitution; and many more are dragged into the work of selling their bodies due to the government policy promoting *kisaeng* tourism. As the Statement of the Women's Forum points out, the Declaration bypasses this shame and lacks repentance of the sin of complicity with patriarchalism and mammonism in the Korean church. The Declaration did contribute to awakening even conservative Christians who did not belong to the member churches of the NCCK to participate in the mission of peace and reunification. But in reality almost all denominations of the Korean church have been earnestly involved in the so-called North Korea mission which aims at recovering each denomination's properties and sending missionaries to build as many denominational churches as possible. This is due to the failure of the Jubilee movement of the Korean church to reform the intra-ecclesiastical structure of patriarchy and mammonism. The Jubilee of peace and reunification will never be achieved by the Holy Spirit movement of the Korean church unless the monopoly of ecclesial power by the elderly male leaders who belong to a Moses' generation is ended. We need a new paradigm of community in which power is shared with the women who are more than seventy percent of the Christian population and with the young men of a Joshua's generation who have played a major role in the democratization of Korea since June 1987.

The new paradigm of the community of Jubilee for interliving is found in the Trinity. In Asia, however, the traditional image of the Trinity can work for the monopoly of patriarchal power in church as well as at home. Asian woman theologians have been suspicious of the complicity of Confucian patriarchy and the Christian Trinity. The male-dominated Trinity of God the Father, God the Son, and God the Holy Spirit cannot illuminate for Asian women in the Confucian patriarchal context the *oikonomia* of God revealed in Jesus Christ. Then what is the image of the Trinity for interliving? Let me share an inspiring symbol I encountered in the "Workshop on Contextual Liturgy and Music" held in Tainan Theological Seminary in January, 1997. Taiwanese Roman Catholic sister Teresa, whom I met in the liturgical dance sub-group, introduced to me the logo of Sprout Group, a Catholic women's concerns group in Taiwan. The logo has three parts which form a circle. A sprouting seed and the four Chinese characters referring to Sprout God are at the top left. At the bottom, three Chinese characters of *nyuh* meaning three women are drawn as if they danced a round dance hand in hand. The logo is shocking to those accustomed to East Asian culture. The Chinese character *ghan*, which consists of three characters of *nyuh* in a triangle, means adultery and sexual immorality. The female trinity in Confucian culture indicates the most derogatory sin of woman. Even when a man commits adultery, his act is still referred to as *ghan*, three women in a triangle. Teresa explained the logo as follows:

> Sprouting seed nestles in the space created by three women holding hands and dancing a celebration of life. The four characters of Sprout Group continue the nurturing circle. The open space around the sprout extends an invitation to all--women and men--who wish to join hands to complete the circle, committing themselves to reflection and action on women-concerns.[11]

132

The image of three women joining hands and dancing deconstructs the patriarchally imposed aversion to woman and reconstructs the liberated and liberating image of woman. The image could become a metaphor of the open Trinity or the Trinity for interliving. The Trinity for interliving is the Trinity of God the (motherly) Father, God the Son (and the Daughter), and the Holy Spirit (the Mother).

God the motherly Father is Jesus' *Abba*-Father.[12] Jesus reveals the *Abba* mystery of God to us, and in the Spirit of freedom we enter into the intimacy of his relationship with God and can also pray, "*Abba*! Father!" (Romans 8:15). Jesus' *Abba*-Father who frees us is distinguished from the world patriarch of Father religion who subjugates us in the spirit of fear. Jesus' *Abba*-Father is no longer the God of patriarchal monotheism but the motherly Father who both begets and gives birth to God the Son and the Daughter.

God the Son and the Daughter is Jesus Christ the Lord and the Servant.[13] The mystery of the two natures of Christ is analogous to the mysterious harmony of the heavenly world of the Father and the earthly world of the Mother (Spirit) in Christ. "There is neither male nor female in Christ Jesus" (Gal. 3:28) because Jesus Christ is God the Son and the Daughter. There is neither slave nor free because Jesus Christ is God the Lord and the Servant. In Jesus Christ, *yin* in *yang*--anima--the woman in man, and *yang* in *yin*--animus--the man in woman, are reconciled.

The Holy Spirit the Mother is the Paraclete, the Comforter who comforts us "as a mother comforts her child" (Isaiah 66: 13). In the womb of the Spirit the believers are reborn. Unless a person is born of water in the womb of the Holy Spirit the Mother, he or she cannot enter the kingdom of God (John 3:5). Corporeal life is affirmed and cared for by the Mother, for the body is "a temple of the Holy Spirit" (1 Corinthians 6:20). The Holy Spirit the Mother "intercedes for us with groans that words cannot express" (Romans 8: 26) and kindly removes our sackcloth and clothes us with joy (Psalm 30:11). Anticipating the resurrection of our bodies as well as of the dead ones, we are touched and moved by the fuzzy beat of the Spirit which turns our wailing into dancing.

We are all invited to the trinitarian's *perichoresis* (round dancing) for interliving. The circle of the round dancing of God the motherly Father, God the Son and the Daughter, and the Holy Spirit the Mother is not closed but open to women and men, slaves and free, the yellow and the white, heaven and earth, and so forth. How can we participate in trinitarian round dancing for interliving in the interkilling situation of our world?

"Like a Seed Which Grows into a Tree" was the theme of the 1997 World Day of Prayer. Korea Church Women United created a liturgy

133

reflecting the suffering of division and the hope of reunification. All the Christian women of the world worshiped with this liturgy. It was an occasion of sharing the ecumenical motif of Jubilee. Kim Yong-nim's theme painting is impressive. A woman in white cloth, crouching and kneeling for prayer, is inside a seed. She holds a bud which is connected to a large tree embracing the earth. Many birds fly into the tree. The image of the woman in a seed corresponds with the biblical interpretation of the Korean women liturgists. They interpret Mark 4:2-9 (the parable of the sower) in the context of suffering Korean women *si-al*.

> We are seeds which have been given Good News. These seeds are sown in the world to actualize liberation, the integrity of creation and world peace.[14]

This interpretation is greatly contrasted with the traditional, allegorical interpretation according to which the seed is the Good News and the soil is the heart of a believer. For Korean women, they themselves are seeds which have been given the Good News and the soil is their life world. This paradigmatic change in understanding the text is possible because Korean women do theology by bodily experience as well as by intellectual concepts.

> Some seeds fell on the hard road where they could not sprout. In Korea this very road is called the Demilitarized Zone which was established fifty-two years ago by powerful countries to divide North and South Korea. For the Comfort Women who were drafted for military sexual slavery by Japan, this hard road is called the road of *han*, sorrow, suffering and death. When the road is hard, our seeds can not even sprout and thus will die."[15]

There are also other stories of the seeds falling on "stony ground where women's worth and dignity were ignored and despised by the patriarchal and Confucian society" and of the seeds falling among "thorn bushes where people only live for their own happiness and well-being without caring for their suffering neighbors." These stories are the social biography of Korean women *si-al*. They have sought good soil. The good soil cannot be given without suffering and struggle. Only the Holy Spirit can give them the power to cultivate it.

> We want our society to be one where righteousness flows like a river. We want a fertile soil where women and men are treated as equals. We want to share the fruits of reunification together. The farmers are anticipating the

harvest and are ready to celebrate the harvest festival with gladness. Only the Holy Spirit can give us the power to realize such a society. Then God's kingdom will come to this earth.[16]

Only the Holy Spirit can give them the power! Such power has made Korean women *si-al* able to survive the barren soil of divided Korea and "break up the fallow ground" (Hosea 10:12) to become the partners of the triune God. Since they believed that God "purposely chose what the world considers the least in order to shame the strong," they earnestly pray, "Lord God, be with us as we strive to live compassionately with the weak." Praising God, who made them one in Christ, they dedicate themselves to enduring their sufferings as the body of Christ. Korean Christian women, who decide to participate in the *oikonomia* of God who continues the new creation of history and the cosmos, are the ones who invite all of us to the trinitarian *perichoresis* of God for interliving. Despite living in the still divided and interkilling world, we are obliged to be open to "New Encounter" for peace and interliving brought by the power of the Holy Spirit.

> Like a seed grows into new bud by meeting with the earth,
> You and I'll become new people by meeting each other.
> Like the heaven creates a new day by meeting with the earth,
> You and I'll become a new creation by meeting each other.[17]

---

1) Cf. *Chundogyo Scripture* (Seoul: Chundogyo Center, 1988).

2) Kim Ji-ha, *Life and Self-government* (Seoul: Sol, 1996), 149.

3) L. George Paik, *History of Protestant Missions in Korea: 1832-1910* (New York: Paragon, 1917), 369.

4) Ham Suk-hun, *Korean History in Biblical Perspective* (Seoul: Hangil Press, 1997), 410-411.

5) *Ibid.,* 416.

6) *Ibid.,* 460.

7) *Ibid.,* 446-447.
Cf. *Chundogyo Scripture* (Seoul: Chundogyo Center, 1988).

8) Cf. National Council of Church in Korea, "Declaration of the Churches of Korea on National Reunification and Peace") "the Declaration" in the followings).

9) Cf. "The Declaration".

10) Cf. "Statement of the Women's Forum for the International Christian Consultation on Justice and Peace in Korea" (Inchon, 1988).

11) Cf. "A Logo of Sprout Group: Catholic Women-Concerning Group."

12) Cf. Elisabeth Moltmann-Wendel, Juergen Moltmann, *Humanity in God* (SCM Press, 1983), 89.

13) Cf. Jung Young Lee, *The Trinity in Asian Perspective* (Abingdon Press, 1996), 78.

14) Cf. Korea Church Women United, "1997 World Day of Prayer Worship Service: Like a seed which grows into a tree" ("Worship Service" in the followings).

15) Cf. "Worship Service".

16) Cf. "Worship Service".

17) Cf. "Worship Service".

CHAPTER 10

The Crawling God

1. A New Reading of the Torah in the Wilderness of Our Times

MY EXPERIENCE OF reading the Torah with the ones who are desperately crawling in '3D' reality,[1] the illegally hired foreign migrant workers, has opened my eyes to envision the new horizon of the Korean church and Korean theology in the twenty-first century. In 1995, about ten migrant workers from Nigeria and the Philippines and three Korean Christians, including myself, used to gather every Wednesday night in a smelly gray barracks, which looked like a prison camp, located in one of the factory districts of Yong-in. Finding that the workers gathered though their bodies were exhausted by working more than twelve hours everyday, I felt sorry for them and was challenged by their passionate faith. Those uprooted people, wandering from place to place and gathering to listen to the word of God, reminded me of the diaspora Jews listening to the Torah and praying to God.

Recent studies of the Pentateuch have paid more attention to the literary criticism of the finished form of the edited text than to analysis of the different documents.[2] Some call this attempt a synchronistic literary criticism in comparison with a diachronic analysis of the documents. One of the merits of such an attempt is the shift of theological emphasis from the Exodus event (Exodus 1–18), which had been the center of previous Pentateuch research, to the Sinai pericope (Exodus 19 through Numbers 10), which includes the long-ignored life of the Israelites in the Sinai wilderness. Those interpreters who emphasize the Exodus like to point out that the report of the Exodus and the Sinai pericope were of two different and independant traditions and they were combined in the later stage. Appropriating a particular social science, Gottwald deliberately breaks the unity of the Sinai pericope from Exodus 16–18 to Numbers 10–20 in order to read the Exodus and the entering of the promised land

137

in terms of the realization of Yahweh's community of equality. All of the law codes in Exodus, Leviticus, and Numbers, which were added to the original tradition of Moses, were formed during the period between the monarchy and the post-exilic era. This, however, cannot justify the assumption that the Exodus ought to concentrate on the once-and-for-all liberation by God. Instead one has to inquire how the Sinai pericope, namely, the Sinai detour, was established in the *Sitz-im-Leben* of the post-exilic period during which the last form of the Pentateuch was edited. The course the Israelites took to enter Canaan under the guidance of the mighty hands of God was not a direct line but a long detour of wandering around the wilderness. They traveled on the detour for about 40 years. It means they neither ran nor flew, but walked very slowly, i.e., they 'crawled' from Egypt to Palestine. The God who went with them is the crawling God. Only on the way to the promised land, while wandering the wilderness round and round, can we understand the profound theological significance entangled in the Sinai pericope.

The Sinai pericope begins with the story of the Israelites pitching tents under Mount Sinai after the Exodus. Through Moses' climbing up and down Mount Sinai seven times, God and Israel made the covenant. Coming down to the top of Mount Sinai was a great concession on the part of God, the Creator of heaven and earth. Then God's coming down into the tent of meeting under the mountain was indeed an incredible self-renunciation by God. After the covenant-making between God and Israel (Exodus 19:3–24:8) comes the story of building the tent of meeting for God, who no longer stayed in the mountain but wanted to dwell in the midst of God's own people (Exodus 24:9–40:38). At this point in the Sinai pericope, the covenant-making and even the Exodus became mere preparation for building the sanctuary of God in the midst of the life of the Israelites. From then on God had to dwell in the tent wherever it was pitched by God's people, that is, God had to move with them as if God crawled. Thus when Israel became the captive of her invaders, God also was exiled in the alien land. Indeed, God had to crawl till "the Word became flesh and pitched its tent among us" (John 1:14).

Leviticus 1:1 ("The Lord called to Moses and spoke to him from the tent of meeting") is the turning point when God stops speaking from Mount Sinai and begins speaking from the tent of meeting. Faith centering around the tent of meeting rejects the religion of pseudotranscendence, which was so carried away by the manifestation of divine mystery at the top of the mountain, that it sought to fly into heaven. Leading the disciples who said, "Rabbi, it is good for us to be here," down the Mount of Transfiguration, Jesus lived together with sinners, healing a boy with an evil spirit. Jesus was a man of faith rooted in the tradition of the tent of meeting. The tent of meeting is not a temple. The Aaronites are frequently mentioned in Leviticus. During the monarchy, however, the Zadokites held the hegemony of the Jerusalem temple. The prophets severely criticized temple religion which limited God to the temple and imprisoned the worshipers by the hierocratic apparatus based on artificial doctrines and institutions.

> This is what the Lord says: "Heaven is my throne/ and the earth is my footstool./ Where is the house you will build for me?/ Where will my resting place be?/ Has not my hand made all these things,/ and so they came into being?"/ declares the Lord./ This is the one I esteem:/ he who is humble and contrite in spirit/ and trembles at my word. (Isaiah 66:1-2)

When Jeremiah prophesied, having gone through the destruction of the Jerusalem temple after the fall of the monarchy, that the new covenant would be written on the hearts of the people of God (Jeremiah 31:33), when Jesus claimed that his body is the temple while he cleared his Father's house which was turned into a market (John 2:13-22), and when Paul asserted that the body of every Christian in whom Christ is present is a temple of the Holy Spirit (1 Corinthians 6:19), they took into consideration the failure of temple religion in the history of Israel.

Reflecting on the failure of temple religion which fell into complicity with the unjust monarchy, Leviticus suggests a new vision of community around the tent of meeting in which people live with God and the rule of God (theocracy) is realized. The tent of meeting is neither a place to escape from reality by flying full speed into the beyond or the future, nor a place to compromise with reality by prostrating oneself for egotistic survival, but a place for the transformation of reality as well as for change of the self to crawl with God in the history of suffering. Having been excluded from the presiding role in temple worship during the monarchy, the Aaronites committed themselves to faith centering around the tent of meeting, which was an alternative to the dilemma between the religion of false transcendence at the mountain top and the temple religion of idolatry. The period during which they edited Leviticus, the Sinai pericope, and even the Pentateuch as a whole was the dark and tragic exilic and post-exilic era. The editing of the Pentateuch was accomplished during the period of the loss of land, nation, and temple. It was done to recover faith in God as well as land and nation. The reason the Sinai pericope was located in the Pentateuch is found in the Aaronite vision of the survival and hope of exilic and post-exilic Israel. This survival would come through supporting the tent of meeting not the temple, the Aaronites not the Zadokites, and the total sanctification of life and cosmos as permanent liberation not once-and-for-all liberation and redemption. Wholeheartedly embracing the tragic reality, those who envisioned the community around the tent of meeting avoided any escape either to the above or to the front. They dared to travel back toward the time of their ancestors who wandered the wilderness after the Exodus in order to crawl with God over the history of suffering, liberation, and sanctification. It was not simply going back to the past, but going 'back to the future'; i.e., it was crawling with God over the '3D' reality, bringing a new dimension of liberated and sanctified life. If the Passover is the festival celebrating the Exodus, the Feast of the Shelters celebrating post-Exodus life in the tents in the wilderness might be called the 'Crawlover'. The Passover refers to God's destroyer passing over the doorways of every Israelite house in Egypt when the destroyer saw the blood of the lamb on the top and sides of the door frame (Exodus 12:23). The Crawlover, then, refers to God's covenant people crawling over the suffering life in the wilderness, keeping the commandments of God in the tent life of every Israelite household. The Passover refers to the redemption and liberation of the Israelites by the grace of the almighty God alone. The Crawlover indicates the sanctification and calling of the people of God who participate in the salvific work of God.

> The Lord said to Moses, "Speak to the entire assembly of Israel and say to them: 'Be holy because I, the Lord your God, am holy'" (Leviticus 19:1-2).

The spirituality of the Feast of the Shelters, the spirituality of the Crawlover, is the spirituality of the unity of worship in the tent of meeting, where the Spirit of God is present, and the daily life of the people in their tents (Leviticus 11-18). And it is also the spirituality of the liberation and sanctification of all lives in the market and the cosmos in relation to the sacred assemblies such as the Sabbath, the Sabbatical Year, and the Year of Jubilee (Leviticus 19-17).

According to Leviticus 11-18, not only the worship of God in the tent of meeting but also daily life in the tents are the means for realizing permanent liberation after the Exodus. The significance of Leviticus for the creative formation of Korean theology of the Spirit could be illuminated in light of a movement of thought and community called Donghak, which emerged in Korea in the middle of the nineteenth century. Initially developed by Choe Je-u and then by his disciple Choe Si-hyong, Donghak (Eastern Way) sought to withstand elements of the Western Way associated

140

with formal colonialistic Christianity represented at that time by Roman Catholicism. The Donghak movement became in time the Donghak Peasant Revolution against concrete structures of oppression whereby the ruling class exploited the *minjung*. Essential to this movement was the insistence that heaven and earth meet in the concrete presence of each and every life as well as of the other person. The other person, or each and every life, was to be seen as the bearer of heaven or God *(si-chun-ju)*. As such the obeisance rendered to the divine (or by the *minjung* to the ruling class and especially the king) was to be rendered to every person (*sa-in-yo-chun* or "treat people as though they were God"). This concretely meant the practice of obeisance to persons of the underclass including women, children, and slaves. The recognition of the other as the bearer of the divine had revolutionary potential. In fact, it issued in revolution and remains till today as the historical irruption of the *minjung* as the subject of history.

In 1897, three years after the failure of the Peasant Revolution because of the intervention of Japanese military forces, Choe Si-hyung called for a liturgical reform called *hyang-ah-sul-wi* (set the ancestral tablet toward the self) while he taught a few peasants in a small village just before he was arrested and hanged by the government. *Hyang-ah-sul-wi* is the opposite of *hyang-byuk-sul-si* (set the ancestral tablet toward the wall). *Hyang-byuk-sul-si* is the age-old Confucianist rule of ancestor worship, setting the ancestral tablet at the altar against the wall and bowing before the rice bowl arranged in front of the tablet. Eighteenth century Catholics first challenged the ideology of ancestor worship in East Asia. Korean Catholic Yun Ji-chung dared to burn his ancestral tablet and tried to send a secret letter to the French fleet in China to retaliate against the Korean government. Yun was beheaded. Catholic martyr Chung Ha-sang criticized ancestor worship: "Though one cannot feed the spirit of a living person with rice and alcohol, how in the world can one feed the spirit of a dead ancestor? How can one serve such a thing like an ancestral tablet as if it were parents?"s[3]

It was no wonder that the early Korean Catholics' rejection of ancestor worship was considered s fundamental challenge to the foundational ideology of Confucian society resulting in more than ten thousand Catholics becoming martyrs in 1791. The iconoclastic mission of Roman Catholicism, however, received backlash even among the *minjung,* who had been permeated with the Confucianist ethos of filial piety. In its initial stage, Donghak was suspected of being another form of Western Learning (Roman Catholicism) mainly because it used the same name of the deity, namely, *chun-ju* (the Heavenly Lord). It was

141

the *via media* of Donghak that appealed to the *minjung*. The were seeking *kae-byuk* (new heaven and new earth) as they faced a double predicament: domestically, the oppression of the corrupt government, and internationally, the invasion of Western and Japanese imperialistic powers. While keeping their faith in God in the typically East Asian form *(si-chun-ju,* each and every being as the bearer of the Heavenly Lord), Donghak revised the Confucian rite of ancestor worship in harmony with its doctrine of God (*hyang-ah-sul-wi,* set the ancestral tablet toward the self).

Hyang-ah-sul-wi, the change from the altar toward the wall to the table toward the self, was actually an authentic revolution of all religious sacrifice in the sense that every person, regardless of his or her social, racial, and sexual background, is the bearer of God, the ultimate ground of all beings including one's ancestors. It was Choe Si-hyung who radicalized the thought of *si-chun-ju* to include all beings in the cosmos as the bearers of God *(chun-ji-man-mul-mak-bi-chi-chun-ju-ya).* It was also Choe Si-hyung whose non-violent resistance movement, based on the equality of all lives, achieved the March 1st Independence Movement in 1919 in solidarity with Korean Protestant Christians. The March 1st Movement, in turn, influenced the May 4th Movement in China and Gandhi's non-violent movement for independence. It is worth quoting Kim ha's contemporary interpretation of Choe Si-hung's thought:

> If *Hyang-byuk-sul-wi* (set the ancestral tablet toward the wall) refers to the basic style of culture that fulfills the demonic monopoly of the rice of life by means of making a crack between the worshiper and the worshiped, *hyang-ah-sul-wi* (set the ancestral tablet toward the self) means the proclamation of *kae-byuk* (new heaven and new earth) by means of making a crack against the crack. Changing the position of the rice bowl from the altar against the wall to the table in front of the self, *hyang-ah-sul-wi* becomes the proclamation of the crack of the *minjung* or of life against the crack of devils which has been fixed between the worshiper and the worshiped for many thousand years. This accords with the revolutionary style of the proclamation of new Sabbath is relation to 'rice'.
>
> Jesus called himself 'rice'' and 'rice'' is the essence of the Mass and of the Eucharist. Rice is the essence of *hyang-ah-sul-wi* as well as of Jesus' Passover Meal and his Crucifixion. In rice the core of *hyang-ah-sul-wi* in Donghak accords with Jesus' proclamation of new Sabbath.[4]

Hyang-byuk-sul-wi (set the ancestral tablet toward the wall) is the form of sacrifice according to which God, the heaven, and the promised land are in the direction of the wall, of my opposite side, and in the future.

Tomorrow demands the *minjung* to endure, sacrifice, abolish, and make void today by bringing the fruits of one's labor, one's dreams, and one's hope and bowing in the direction of the wall and of the future. *Hyang-byuk-sul-wi* also operates in the capitalist market economy which promises the *minjung* enormous panic, labor-management disputes, and ecological crises. The spirit of the text, which thoroughly treats what one can eat and what one should not eat in the daily diet (Leviticus 11:1-47), is the unity of meal and sacrifice. Leviticus is in accord with Choe Si-hyung's teaching on the matter of revering life through keeping the unity of meal and sacrifice.

> Do not eat any of the fat of cattle, sheep or goats. Anyone who eats the fat of an animal from which an offering by fire may be made to the Lord must be cut off from his people.(Leviticus 7:23, 25)
> You must not eat the blood of any creature, because the life of every creature is its blood; anyone who eats it must be cut off.(Leviticus 17:14).
> Do not mix left-over rice with new rice, left-over soup with new soup, left-over *kimchi* with new *kimchi*, left-over dish with new dish. Keep the left-over rice, soup, *kimchi*, and dish in a separate place and eat them when you are hungry without full prayer but with saying, "I'm eating."
> Do not eat food in a cracked dish or in a dish with jagged edges. Do not kill any life. Enjoy your three daily meals as if you offered sacrifice to your parents.(Naesudomun)

What is the contemporary meaning of the unity of meal and sacrifice or of *hyang-ah-sul-wi*? Nowadays we eat heavily pesticided rice. Recently the meat imported from Nebraska, U.S.A., was infected with 0-157, which is fatal to our life. Organic agriculture and the direct transaction between the producer and the consumer have become a rising concern of many people in Korea. In our era of ecological crisis, the concern for food and health becomes an ultimate concern. This reflects the spirit of *hyang-ah-sul-wi* and of the unity of meal and sacrifice in our times. The teaching of Choe Si-hyung mentioned above was for pregnant women. For Choe the pregnant woman is not only 'the bearer of God' *(si-chun-ju)* but also 'the rearer of God' *(yang-chun-ju)* and 'the enactor of God' *(che-chun-ju)*. And Choe asserts that everyone's calling is the same as the pregnant woman's. The calling of bearing, rearing, and enacting God in our daily life is also found in the guidelines for caring for the skin (Leviticus 13:2-46; 14:1-32), the cleaning of clothes and of the house (Leviticus 13:37-59; 14:33-53), and a pure sex life (Leviticus 15:1-33). Rice is heaven and home is the kingdom of God. Daily life is a holy rite.

2. The Sabbath, the Sabbatical Year and the Year of Jubilee

The spirituality of the Feast of the Shelters as the spirituality of the Crawlover reaches its peak in the Holiness Code (Leviticus 19–27). Beginning with the command of God, "Be holy" (Leviticus 19:2), the Holiness Code includes the directions of God concerning the sanctification of society, cosmos, and history in relation to the Sabbath, the Sabbatical Year and the Year of Jubilee. Compared to the short statement about the Sabbath in Exodus, the Code of the Sabbath in Leviticus covers not only rest from work but also the broad range of the sanctified life, such as concern for the poor and for foreigners (Leviticus 19:9-10, 33-34), the prohibition of the exploitation of labor and of the delayed payment of wages (Leviticus 19:13), and fairness in judgment and trade (Leviticus 19:35-36). Indeed, "the Sabbath was made for man, not man for the Sabbath" (Mark 2:27). The sin of Sabbath breaking is not so much nonattendance at Sunday worship as the violation of the human rights of another person. The following is the story of the predicament of a foreign migrant worker.

> Korean Chinese Lim Ho paid 3,000 dollars to a Chinese broker to come to Korea. After he worked for 18 months, he was arrested by the police and was brought to The Immigration Bureau. Out of 4,000 dollars he made for 18 months, he lent 2,000 dollars to one of his relatives who ran away from his debt. Out of 2,000 dollars left he paid 1,800 dollar fine and only 200 dollars was left with him. By 200 dollars he could not buy air ticket. He bought seafaring ticket and less than 20 dollars was left. After he thought about his debt by which he paid to the broker and worried about returning home broke, he wrote and left his will on the Guroh elevated road on the November 9th of 1993 and jumped from it to finish his life. Who is going to pay for his blood?[5]

There are about two hundred thousand foreign migrant workers in Korea. Korean Christians are enthusiastic about the growing role of the Korean church in overseas missions. But they are rather indifferent to the foreigners living in their neighborhood. God said to the Israelites who mistreated the foreigners among Israel, "When an alien lives with you in your land, do not mistreat him. The alien living with you must be treated as one of your native-born. Love him as yourself, for you were aliens in Egypt. I am the Lord your God" (Leviticus 19:33-34). Just like the Korean saying, "Frog forgets its larval stage," Koreans have forgotten that they lost their nation for thirty-six years under Japanese colonial rule. The have

144

gone through the thorny path of national division for more than a half century, screaming *"Pali, pali!"* ('Fast, fast!' in Korean, which every foreign worker in Korea knows well and with contempt) to the alien brothers and sisters to exploit and oppress them. Just as Jesus cured a man on the Sabbath whose right hand was shriveled (Luke 6:6-11), fighting for the compensation of foreign workers, as well as caring for those who lose their fingers in a press or catapult work and have no medical insurance, is the way Korean Christians keep the law of the Sabbath.

The Code of the Sabbatical Year and of the Year of the Jubilee (Leviticus 25) asserts the sanctification of earth and of history on earth as well as personal sanctification. The Code of the Sabbatical Year (Leviticus 25:1-7) indicates the ecological sensitivity of the editor of Leviticus. The deep meaning of the Sabbatical Year is not the custom of fallowing for better crops but the participation of the land in the rest of God. Through keeping its Sabbath in the seventh year, the land and God live together in rest.

> But in the seventh year the land is to have a Sabbath of rest, a Sabbath to the Lord (Leviticus 25:4a).

Choe Si-hyung considers the land the face of God in his "Naesudomun".

> Do not pour waste water or any water far away, do not spit far away, and do not blow your nose far away. When saliva or snot falls to the ground, wipe it. If you spit, blow your nose and pour water far away, you spit, blow your nose and pour water to the face of the heaven-earth parents. Always remember this and be careful.(Naesudomun)

The land does not have to be deified as *Gaia,* but it has to be revered as the face of God. Choe's thought calls for a paradigmatic shift in spirituality for the integrity of creation. Western Christianity, in complicity with Western imperialism conquering the land of the Third World, has suppressed and distorted the spirituality of earth, mother, and the Crawlover while it has maximized and absolutized the spirituality of heaven, father, and transcendence. It was in 1841 in the land of the Sioux, one of the native North American tribes, that white Catholic priest De Smet presented himself to the chief of the Sioux and used the occasion to put on a liturgical demonstration to which the Sioux responded with a liturgical act of their own:

> I made the sign of the cross and said the prayer. All the time it lasted, all the savage company, following their chief's example, held their hands raised

145

toward heaven; the moment it was ended, they lowered their right hands to the ground. I asked the chief for an explanation of this ceremony. "We raise our hands," he replied, "because we are wholly dependent on the Great Spirit; it is his liberal hand that supplies all our wants. We strike the ground afterward, because we are miserable beings, worms crawling before his face."[6]

George E. Tinker, an Osage/Cherokee, criticizes De Smet's fabrication of the Indian response. Opposing De Smet, who fit the behavior patterns of another culture to his own frame of reference, Tinker reconstructs the Indian response in the light of a fundamental understanding of the Plains Indians" worldview.

> Surely, these Sioux people are respecting and even summoning, in their own prayer act, the spiritual power of the reciprocity of sky and earth, Grandfather and Grandmother, *Tunkasila* and *Unci*, spirit and matter, male and female. Recognizing and respecting the spiritual intent of De Smet's prayer, these people joined him in prayer in the way that they knew. And far from being a self-negating act, the touching of the earth was undoubtedly an act of piety calling on the power of *Wakan Tanka* (God) as it is manifest in Earth.[7]

The Sioux people's spirituality and act of prayer, which revered earth as well as heaven, was distorted by a Western missionary as if they were miserable worms crawling. Such distortion is a form of cultural genocide. Indeed, the Westerners were the ones who made the native people the miserable worms of humankind and forced them to crawl in the suffering history. Even the crawling worms are not miserable beings because they are also the bearers of God. The beautiful spirituality of the Sioux and of Donghak opens up a new perspective of the hitherto ignored dimension of earth, mother, and the Crawlover in Christian spirituality.

St. Paul asserts that Christians, as those who are in Christ, are set free by the law of the Spirit of life from the law of sin and death (Romans 8:1-2). Here the Spirit, as the Spirit of Christ, is the Spirit of God who raised Jesus from the dead and through whom life will be given to the Christians' mortal bodies (Romans 8:9-11). Furthermore, the great privilege of the Christian is that the Spirit herself testifies with our spirit that they are the children of God (Romans 8:15-16). Receiving the Spirit of sonship, Christians become co-heirs with Christ. Therefore, Christians ought to share in the suffering of Christ in order to share in his glory (Romans 8:17). In other words, Christians ought to crawl with God who crawled in Christ and as Christ. According to Paul, unless "the Spirit helps

146

us in our weakness," we cannot crawl with God, i.e., "we do not know what we ought to pray" (Romans 8:26a). Here crawl as "walking humbly and closely with God" is a posture of Christian prayer as well as sharing in the suffering of Christ. And the Spirit of God who crawled in Christ is the Mother "interceding for us with groans that words cannot express" (Romans 8:26b).

> We know that the whole creation has been groaning as in the pains of childbirth right up to the present time. Not only so, but we ourselves, who have the first fruits of the Spirit, groan inwardly as we wait eagerly for our adoption as sons, the redemption of our bodies. . . . In the same way, the Spirit helps us in our weakness. We do not know what we ought to pray, but the Spirit himself intercedes for us with groans that words cannot express.(Romans 8:22-23, 26)

In the above text the maternal nature of the Spirit, who works for the new creation of all creatures, is clearly demonstrated. The communion of the children of God with the groaning creatures is also evident, because the children are the members of the whole creation groaning for liberation. Therefore, the freedom of the children of God and the liberation of the groaning creation are two sides of the same coin. The whole creation, the children of God, and the Mother Spirit groan together in the midst of cosmic suffering for the sake of the new creation. The whole creation groans in the pains of childbirth, waiting in eager expectation for the children of God to be revealed. And the children of God, in turn, groan inwardly as they wait eagerly for their adoption as children of God, the redemption of their bodies. From the beginning until the end of creation the Spirit intercedes for the children of God with groans that words cannot express. The eschatological appearance of the children of God is insepa-rably united with the new creation of the Mother Spirit, groaning as in the pains of childbirth and interceding between her children and God the Father.

The Pauline understanding of salvation has nothing to do with anthro-pocentrism which ignores the integrity of the whole creation. In our times of ecological crisis we may learn from the Mahayana Buddhist ideal of simultaneous attainment of the Way *(dojijodo* in Japanese), referring to "the fact everything in the universe attains enlightenment simultaneously at the moment of one's own enlightenment--an enlightenment that opens up the universal horizon of the Buddha-nature."[8] In the spring of 1997 I attended Aram I, the president of the Central Committee of the World Council of Churches, on his visit to the executive chief of the Korean

147

Buddhist Chogye Order. Walking up the stairs leading to the office of the executive chief, I glimpsed a Chinese chirography of the words of the Order's supreme patriarch: "The Buddha-nature is in every being and even a worm crawling on the floor is my brother." Serving as the interpreter for the dialogue between the two leaders, I was excited when the topic of their discussion moved on to the issue of religion and the ecological crisis. Aram I began to talk about God the Creator's love for the whole creation and the Christian vocation for the integrity of creation. Song Wall-ju, executive chief of the Chogye Order, responded to him in a polite yet straightforward way to point out that there is no God in Buddhism and human beings should not manipulate any being because the Buddha-nature is everywhere. Suddenly I perceived a sharp tension between Christianity and Buddhism represented by the two leaders. As we came out of the office after a rather conventional dialogue, Aram I happened to look at a poster about the Buddha's birthday. The green-colored poster described a large dewed leaf on which a little boy Buddha sits face to face with an indigenous small green frog. Remembering a recent report of the disruption of the ecological equilibrium caused by an unexpected invasion of large American brown frogs, I could immediately perceive the message of the poster. A green leaf, a little frog, and a boy Buddha do not exist separately because each and every one of them has the same Buddha-nature and belongs to one great Life. Being moved as well as amused by the poster, Aram I was all smiles. As he said, "all are brothers in God," the Rev. Song nodded assent with a smile.

If Aram I had more time to discuss his Orthodox understanding of God, he would have pointed out the omnipresence as well as the omnipotence of the motherly God the Father. According to the Eastern Orthodox tradition of the Trinity, God the Father is the motherly God who begets the Son and brings forth the Spirit. John Wesley, whose theology as practical divinity was deeply affected by the Eastern Fathers, also asserts God's gracious presence in and through the Spirit:

> The great God, the eternal, almighty Spirit, is as unbounded in his presence as in his duration and power . . . God acts . . . throughout the whole compass of creation, by sustaining all things, without which everything would sink into its primitive nothing, by governing all, every minute superintending everything . . . strongly and sweetly influencing all, and yet without destroying the liberty of his rational creatures.[9]

It is important to note Wesley's trinitarian understanding of the Spirit keeps the omnipresence of God in a critical tension with the omnipotence of God. The omnipotence of God is not the Creator's arbitrary domination of the creation. Instead, it means that God "transcends and abolishes the ontological necessity of the substance by being God as Father" who is the cause both of the generation of the Son and of the procession of the Spirit.[10] Contrary to ontological monism according to which the being of God and the being of the world are linked together, biblical faith proclaims God to be absolutely free with regard to the world. Yet the freedom of God is not for the Gnostic gulf between God and the world, but for the communion of God with the world. It is not the being of God as a metaphysical concept, such as substance or being itself, but the being of God as person, i.e., as the *hypostasis* of the motherly Father, who out of love freely begets the Son and brings forth the Spirit, that is identical with an act of communion. Therefore, without destroying the liberty of rational creatures, the Mother Spirit strongly and sweetly influences all to help them enter into communion with God the Father. The testimony of the Spirit that we are the children of God the Father ought to be kept alive in between 'already' and 'not yet'. Receiving the Spirit of adoption, we cry, "*Abba,* Father." Participating in the groaning creation, we wait eagerly for our adoption as the children of God, the redemption of our bodies, which is the goal of the Spirit's working with us for the new creation.

The whole creation has been groaning and moaning ever since Adam and Eve began the blood-stained history of humankind. The sanctification of the land cannot be achieved unless the history of the descendants of Adam is sanctified. Without justice and peace, there is no integrity of creation. This is the spirit of the Year of Jubilee (Leviticus 25:8-55). The Year of Jubilee is the year of atonement and reconciliation. It means the realization of the rest of God in human history. In other words, the rest of God 'cracks' and interrupts the flow of forward running development with mad speed. It is significant to notice that the Year of Jubilee starts with the ceremony of atonement. The personal and communal sin of breaking the Sabbath, as well as the Sabbatical Year, for the last forty-nine years are atoned for in the Year of Jubilee. But for such atonement repentance is demanded. Repentance as turning to God is to crawl with God who crawls with the least of living organisms as well as with humankind. This reminds me of reading Genesis 33 with foreign migrant workers in 1995. Through that experience I learned how important it was to make a crack into the 'fast, fast' killing speed in order to live together with the least of the brothers and sisters of Christ.

Looking up at Esau coming with his four hundred men, Jacob went on ahead of his household with fear and trembling and bowed down to the ground seven times as he approached his brother. Jacob had been very quick to take the rights and blessing of the first-born son away from Esau. Jacob had also been very clever in cheating his uncle Laban to increase his own riches. Yes, Jacob had run his life very fast until he returned home. When he heard that Esau was coming with his four hundred men to meet him, Jacob feared and trembled. Furthermore, wrestling with an angel, his hip had been wrenched. Jacob could not run fast any more. When he saw Esau, he bowed down to the ground seven times. Being reconciled with Esau, Jacob even said, "To see your face is like seeing the face of God." Then Esau was so moved by Jacob's kind and polite attitude that he suggested that his younger brother go quickly to his place: "Let us be on our way; I'll accompany you" (Gen. 33:12). Jacob's response to Esau's invitation is rather surprising:

> My lord knows that the children are tender and that I must care for the ewes and cows that are nursing their young. If they are driven hard just one day, all the animals will die. So let my lord go on ahead of his servant, while I move along slowly at the pace of the droves before me and that of the children, until I come to my lord in Seir (Gen. 33:13-14).

According to the Chinese classic *Lao-tzu*, *"saeng-I-bul-yu, jang-I-bu-jae"* (As they are born, do not own them; as they grow up, do not control them). Whether they are your children or your cattle, you should not mistreat them because they are the bearers of heaven. Reverence for life is impossible if one tries to own and control it. Reverence for life is possible only when one opens a holy crack between one and the other. Opening a crack in his too speedy life in order to make room for the others, Jacob inverted the domination of economic value over life value. Jacob did move along slowly at the pace of the crawling droves. No wonder Jacob is called Israel. The God of Israel is the God who proclaims his Sabbath in history. Yes, the God of Jacob and of Israel is God crawling with the least of humankind as well as of all living beings.

The Korean church of the last fifty years looks after Jacob, the fast runner. It has been well known all over the world that the Korean church has been the fastest growing church and the largest local church in the world is in Seoul. The Korean church has sent more than three thousand missionaries to more than 120 countries. Recently, however, the growth of the Korean church reached its plateau and some serious symptoms of negative growth appeared. For instance, the above mentioned local church is reported to have lost more than thirty thousand members in 1996. If most of the charismatic pastors of the mammoth churches retire within ten years, the continuing growth of such churches will not be guaranteed.

Many pastors and theologians are talking about the crisis of the Korean church. Could this crisis mean both danger and opportunity? How can we seize the opportunities offered to us and shape them creatively?

The main cause of the crisis in the Korean church is, paradoxically, the fast growth of the Korean church.[11] It has cost faithful discipleship and social credibility. The emphasis on blessing in the church growth movement has secularized the Korean church. In fact, the principles of business administration are applied to the numerical growth of local churches. A theology of blessing was effective in times of fast economic growth. When most Christians became middle class, their needs became more sophisticated than material blessings and success. Middle class people want to rest from their highly competitive way of life. Many leisure industries attract them. The church-goers among them are not ready for the hard message of costly discipleship. Furthermore, non-Christian and even Christian residents in a town tend to oppose starting a new church in their neighborhood because a residential area with a church is considered noisy and crowded, and the price of the real estate in the area definitely goes down. The Korean church has lost touch with local communities.

Overcoming this crisis in the Korean church demands not a new program for church growth but a fundamental change of ecclesiastical understanding and praxis. Just as Jacob became Israel when he turned to God, not only by acknowledging the face of his brother as the face of God and but also by going slowly with the pace of the crawling droves and of the children, the Korean church ought to turn to God by embracing the North Korean people on the one hand and by living together with the other people in the multinational, religiously plural world on the other. The Holy Spirit movement of the Korean church for the twenty-first century must be the Jubilee movement for both the peaceful reunification of Korea and peaceful and just interliving in the midst of ethnic, national and religious conflicts. Therefore, the Jubilee Year of the Korean church has to go beyond the boundary of the Korean nation. It must become the ecumenical Jubilee in the genuine sense of that word. After the fall of the USSR, ethnicity has re-emerged as a major cause of many wars and violence. Even in Korea, where the ghost of the Cold War era is still dominant, the presence of foreign migrant workers is challenging the hitherto homogeneous nation-state. In Korea, as well as in the world today, the forces of integration and disintegration are in strong confrontation with each other. The slowing down of Korean church growth is not so much a gloomy crisis as a new opportunity for Korean Christians to learn a genuinely ecclesial way of life, that is, interliving or living together in mission. Such new birth of the Korean church is possible only when she voluntarily slows down the ambitious speed of numerical growth in order to go at the pace of the least of the brothers and sisters of Christ. If we reflect upon the history of the suffering Korean *minjung* overseas, most of whom, living in Japan, China, the United States, and Russia, had to leave their home country during the tragic period of colonial rule and the war, we can not mistreat the strangers doing the '3D' work in Korea today. As a matter of fact, Korean Christians' past experiences of suffering and hard work overseas might become fruitful resources for imaginative ministry and mission on behalf of the least brothers and sisters of Christ. The Korean church, if she obeys the call for the Jubilee, is the best candidate for the mission of repentance and reconciliation in a world divided by economic, ethnic, and religous differences. Now is the time of God's favor, now is the day of salvation. Let's crawl with God!

---

1) The '3D' reality refers to the situation of foreign migrant workers in Korea who are hired for the kind of work that is difficult, dangerous, and dirty.

2) Cf. Tai-il Wang's unpublished paper for the Biblical Studies Working Group of the Tenth Oxford Institute, August 12-22, 1997, "Reading the Composition of the Pentateuch in a Wesleyan Tradition."

3) Park Keun-won, ed., *Christianity and Confucian Rites* (Seoul: Jeonmangsa, 1985), 80.

4) Kim Ji-ha, *Rice* (Seoul: Bundo Publishing House, 1993), 87.

5) Cf. The N.C.C.K., *Church and World*, August, 1995.

6) George E. Tinker, *Missionary Conquest: The Gospel and Native American Cultural Genocide* (Minneapolis: Augsburg Fortress, 1993), 13.

7) Ibid., 14.

8) Masao Abe, *Zen and Western Thought* (Hong Kong: The Macmillian Press, 1985), 42.

9) Quoted from Albert C. Outler's *"A Focus on the Holy Spirit: Spirit and Spirituality in John Wesley,"* *Quarterly Review*, Vol. 8, No. 2, 1988, 14.

10) John D. Zizioulas, *Being as Communion: Studies in Personhood and Church* (Crestwood: St. Vladmir's Seminary Press, 1993), 44.

11) Cf. Lee Won-gue, "A Socialogical Study on the Factors for Church Growth and Decline in Korea," *Theology and World*, Vol. 34, Spring, 1997.

CHAPTER 11

Dance in the Spirit!

1. A story of my life

I WAS BORN in 1954 right after the Korean War (1950-53). My parents were second generation Methodists. I grew up in an evangelical community near Seoul. My church was located in Gupabal, a small town which used to be a horse station in the old days. My town belongs to Shindo province where a lot of Shamans resided. When my family moved into the area, there was only a Presbyterian church. My parents became the founding members of the Jin Kwan Methodist Church in the town. The name Jin Kwan came from the old Buddhist temple in the area. I was active in the youth group of the church and entered a high school established by the Korean Presbyterian Church. I had my born-again experience when I was 17 years old and I was proud of my Christian identity.

My first encounter with Shamanism was comic as well as tragic. Nearby my house there was a divine tree several hundred years old under and around which the village folks gathered to have their *kut* (Shamanistic ritual). One day when I was about 13 years old, there was great *kut* under the tree. Many people came to participate in it. A famous Shamaness was there to lead the *kut* and everything was set up, including a boiled pig's head stuck to the spearhead at the altar. The scene was disgusting to me, a self-anointed iconoclast. I and a few of my friends went up to a small mountain at the foot of which the divine tree stood. My heart trembled with prophetic rage and I threw a couple of stones at the Shamanistic altar. My mother used to tell her church members proudly that one of the stones her son threw hit the pig's head and the *kut* was messed up. Several years later I happened to look at a middle age woman weeping under the divine tree. I heard that the woman lost her son in the Army. I did not know (and even I suspect she knew) the exact cause of his death. Koreans call the agonized pain of the wounded soul, such as this woman had, *han*, the feeling rooted in the depth of a suffering heart. At that time I was too young

153

and naive to understand *han*. Whenever I played with my friends on the ground of the valley in my village, we saw the skulls and bones of those who were killed during the Korean War. At the time I was only afraid of bad dreams without knowing why those people were killed. Yes, I did see the woman weeping and the skulls deserted. But I could not and would not listen to their *han* cry. As the divine tree withered, the village *kut* also disappeared. And the ghosts of the dead did not appear any more at the haunted house after a devout Christian family moved in.

As I recall my past spiritual journey, one thing I regret is my encounter with Pentecostalism. It was in 1979, when I served as an assistant Army chaplain of the battalion stationed near the Demilitarized Zone, that I began to speak in tongues. I had been cynical about Pentecostalism for a long time and never even imagined myself speaking in crazy sounds. The prayer mountain of the Full Gospel Church was near my battalion. From time to time I visited there with my colleague chaplain assistants and discovered many people sick either in body or in soul. I did pray in the mountain and sing hymns with the people. Yet I still considered Pentecostalism a retreat from the real world and I thought I was too rational to receive any spiritual signs. One day I fell asleep in the barracks chapel of my battalion and dreamt a mysterious dream. In the dream I discovered that the light in the chapel was completely gone, and I saw my own head broken into two pieces. I was so scared that I trembled and tried to pray aloud as I woke up from the dream. A few minutes later I realized that I was speaking in tongues. I suspect my experience of the Spirit was an outcome of the severe environment of my military life. As a matter of fact, I dreamt many bad dreams, even after I got out of the Army.

My theological dislike of Pentecostalism and my religiously proud attitude toward Shamanism somehow coincided. Both of them are the religious movements of the underprivileged. Yet they can be easily distorted to become reactionary ideologies when their manipulators turn from the oppressed into the oppressors. It was not so much the popular dimension of Korean Pentecostal Shamanism as its manipulation by the elites that I had been cynical about for a long time. I had been wandering in the barren wilderness of both liberals and fundamentalists since I entered seminary. I was too rational to be a Pentecostal and not rational enough to be an atheist. I was fed up with the lukewarm state of my soul and I could not stand my own theology, even though I continued doing theology as usual. Because what I theologized was not what I felt deep in my soul driven by the Spirit, it led to my theological self-alienation. I don't think the Pentecostal Shamanists in Korea have the kind of anxiety that I have had. The interkilling law of modern Western two-beat theology reflects the endless conflict between liberal historicism, which reduces the historically unprovable Christian faith into a mere myth, and conservative fundamentalism, which suffocates free criticial thinking. In such a situation what one needs is not merely new theological thinking in one's head but an experience of one's spiritual breakthrough renewing one's guts. I want to construct a theology of the Spirit as a three-beat theology that includes the evangelical-Pentecostal experience, the *minjung*-liberation perspective and the indigenization-dialogical concern for religious-cultural pluralism. What is most uniquely Korean in my theology ought to be derived from the genuine character of the Korean Christian church.

2. Goodbye, Neo-neo-Confucianism!: A Jonah in the Belly of the Dragon Called the System of Division

Struggling between my evangelical faith background and my teachers' ecumenical theology during my Seminary years (1973-1977), my eyes were gradually opened up to discover the reality of my divided nation. The division was not only a political-ideological reality but also a religious-cultural reality. Yun Sung-bum, one of my teachers, played the leading role in the construction of Korean theology in relation to the Christian-neo-Confucian dialogue. The ideal of the sage in Confucianism lies in "cosmotheandric intuition" (Ramond Panikkar). According to the Confucian classic, *Chung Yung XXII*, "The only supreme sincerity of heaven and earth can carry the inborn nature of others to its fulfillment; getting to the bottom of the natures of men, one can thence understand the nature of material things, and this understanding of the nature of things can aid the transforming and nutritive powers of earth and heaven (ameliorate the quality of the grain, for example) and raise the human to be a sort of third partner with heaven and earth." Here sincerity is not limited to human virtue; it is also the way (*Tao*) of heaven and earth. Because of the only supreme sincerity in heaven and earth, nature came to be in its 'suchness' (a Zen-Buddhist term referring to 'as-it-isness' or true nature), and human beings and all beings in the world can participate in the harmony of heaven and earth. *Sung*, the only supreme sincerity of heaven and earth, which is the highest ideal of Confucian sages, consists of two Chinese characters, *un* which means "word" and *sung* which means "to accomplish." Yun interprets the Confucian metaphor of sincerity in terms of the accomplished Word.[1] Considering Jesus Christ to be the phenomenon of the only supreme sincerity, Yun attempts to build his cosmotheandric Christology. The Confucian metaphor of heavenly sincerity and the Biblical faith in the faithfulness of God are not same. Yet, if one tried to interpret the original revelation of Jesus Christ in the Confucian culture, one needs the kind of dialogical imagination that brings both the Eastern religious classics and the Bible together to envision the new horizon of the Christian faith in Asia. The cosmic Christ has been present in the wisdom traditions of the East in unknown ways, so that the clear manifestation of Jesus as the Christ could be achieved by the mission and evangelism of the Asian churches.

The cosmotheandric vision is deeply rooted in the *yin-yang* symbol which is derived from the Confucian classic, *I Ching*. Most East Asian philosophies could be described as only commentaries on this classic. The *yin-yang* symbol is the symbol of harmonious change. The *yin* is the dark principle which is correlated with the moon. The *yang* is the light symbol which is correlated with the sun. When the creative *yang* and the receptive *yin* interact, change occurs. *Yin* always changes to *yang* by union, *yang* changes to *yin* by separation. Union occurs through the expansion of *yin* and separation through the contraction of *yang*. The alteration of expansion and contraction or growth and decay makes possible the union of the separated and the separation of the united. When things have expanded to their maximums, they must contract. When they have contracted to their minimums, they must expand again. Perhaps one of the most outstanding embodiments of the *yin-yang* principle is Tai-Chi exercise. In Tai-Chi exercise *yin* is softness and emptiness and *yang* is toughness and substance. Through Tai-Chi exercise one can participate in the cosmic harmony of heaven and earth. Your soul as well as your body become completely attuned to the cosmic flow of harmonious change. Just like the alteration of *yin* and *yang* in cosmic changes, your body moves with the *yin-yang* rhythm of softness and toughness and of emptiness and substance. The harmony of *yin* and *yang*, however, was constantly abused by the oppressive rulers in the Confucian tradition and it turned out to be a suppressive ideology of domination that sanctioned the inequality between man and woman, between the old and the young, and between the ruler and the ruled. There was no harmony in Confucian socio-history. *Minjung* sought harmony against harmony.

The sublime Confucian, as well as Buddhist and Taoist, ideal of the sage, based on the cosmotheandric intuition, will remain a 'meta-cosmic' speculation unless it becomes down-to-earth through the liberation of the suffering *minjung* in the cosmic arena. No matter how noble and sublime the ideal could be, such spirituality uprooted from Asian soil is nothing but theological orientalism, which perpetuates an affluent leisure class with a pseudospirituality of mental tranquility and physical fitness on the one hand and endorses an apolitical escape from the reality of the suffering

Asian *minjung* on the other. There is no short cut to the cosmotheandric vision. Nobody can escape this history full of unjustifiable evil and unbearable suffering. The earth you step on, the heaven you stare at, and the people you live with have become not harmonious but victimized by the dreadful system of interkilling, i.e., the structural evil and the organized sin that keep most Asians suffering. Only when you can listen to the *han*-cry of the earth, human beings, and even the Spirit of God, can you crawl over this history of suffering and sin just as the Lord Jesus did. Therefore, do not start your cosmotheandric dance before you crawl with God and the suffering ones.

My teacher Yun's theology was progressive in the sense that it participated in the boom of Korean studies in the 1960s. But it was problematic in the sense that it lacked the prophetic function to criticize the emerging political dictatorship called Korean democracy in the 1970s. The movements of students, intellectuals, and labor workers for the democratization of Korean society opened my eyes to the issues of sociopolitical theology. At that time college students' performance of the traditional mask dance was not simply a cultural activity but political resistance. The government forced all high school and college students to go through weekly military training. From high school to seminary I received military training and I was drafted by the Korean Army after I graduated from the seminary. I served in the battalion near the Demilitarized Zone for twenty-seven months. After ten years I was so used to close order drill that I tended to march even after I became a civilian. Indeed, I preferred marching to dancing. In any case, dancing was a sensual and immoral sin for a pious person like me. The very process of my change from a marching soldier to a dancing theologian characterizes my spiritual journey of searching for the creative formation of a Korean theology of the Spirit.

The militarization of society was caused by the late president Park's developmental dictatorship which violated the human rights of many laborers by the policy of low wages and fast economic growth on the one hand and democracy crushed to death for the sake of national security on the other. It was after I was discharged from the service, when the Kwangju massacre took place in 1980, that I was able to identify the fundamental cause of military dictatorship with the system of division. And only recently, as South Korea faced "IMF shock" in 1997, did I thoroughly realize that the system of division is a part of the world capitalist system. Applying Wallerstein's world system theory to the Korean situation, Paik Nak-chung asserts that the system of division is a subdivision of the world system.[2] The contradiction in the system of division does not lie in the interstate relation between North Korea and South Korea, instead it lies between the status quo of the two states and the *minjung* of North and South Korea. The system of division is the system of conflict between the two quasi nation-states which justify themselves by the rhetoric of national reunification. In 1972 the North and South governments declared the July 4th communique to affirm the three principles of peace and reunification, i.e., independence, peace, and national solidarity. Ironically, however, both governments solidified the system of division throughout the 1970s. In the South, Park launched the so-called *Yu-shin* (restoration) system which looked after the *Meiji* emperor system in order to seize permanent political power. In the North, the personal worship of Kim Il-sung began in the name of *Ju-che* (subjecthood) thought. Despite their ideological differences, both regimes used the Confucian ethos of loyalty and filial piety to rationalize their authoritarian totalism.

I would like to call the system of division, which is a subsystem of the world system, neo-neo-Confucian. Neo-neo-Confucianism is not neo-Confucianism, which was the dominant ideology of the last premodern Chosun dynasty from the fifteenth century to the nineteenth century. The failure to have a smooth transition from the premodern society of the peasants to the modern industrial society in Korea was caused by the reactionary regime suppressing any structural reform as well as by the colonial powers of the West and Japan. The watershed between neo-Confucianism and neo-neo-Confucianism was the Donghak revolution in 1894, which was brutally suppressed by the Japanese, and thus the historic chance of creatively overcoming the neo-Confucian ideology was lost. The neo-Confucian regime was merely replaced by the Japanese colonial regime, and the Korean *minjung*'s great yearning for a new world was distorted and repressed. The world capitalist system operated in Korea through Japanese rule. The historical process through which the reactionary forces became pro-Japanese lackeys, and later pro-American lackeys, is the historical process of the formation of the neo-neo-Confucian system of division as a subsystem of the world system.

In the history of the modern West, patriarchal power was abolished for the sake of the institutionalization of fraternal democracy. If the history of Western political thought is the history of patricide, the history of Korean politics is the history of fratricide out of which neo-neo-Confucian patriarchy was constantly restored. Despite so many foreign invasions and peasant uprisings, the neo-Confucian regime survived for almost five centuries by suffocating the messianic imagination of the *minjung*. According to a legend from North Pyung-ahn, the neo-Confucian regime hunted down a "baby generalissimo."

158

Writer Choi Yin-hoon dramatized the legend in his play, *Good Old Days, Shoo Shoo*. The setting of his play was the old time of severe famine when the people of a mountain village heard the cry of the dragon-horse, which was the sign of the coming of a baby generalissimo. The baby boy was born in a poor mumbling peasant's home and he spoke before he learned to crawl. The baby's father suffocated him in the original version of the legend. But in Choi's play the dead baby was resurrected and rode on the dragon-horse with his parents. The village folks gestured as if they shooed birds away while the policemen looked at the flying family as if "a dog failed to chase a chicken."

policeman 1	Where did they go?
policeman 2	Are you sure?
policeman 1	Yes, last night the baby had convulsions.
policeman 3	Well.
horseman 1	They came back after they buried the baby in the mountain.
horseman 2	Look at that.
people	Oh, look!
	All three of them are riding on dragon-horse, flying up in heaven.
	They are throwing flowers at us
	When you arrive in heaven, tell the heavenly Lord, please don't send a generalissimo to our village again.
	As everyone takes turn to speak, from heaven
from heaven	our baby
	sweet baby
people	Shoo! Never come back, shoo! Shoo! (as if they were shooing birds)
from heaven	It has to grow up,
	drinking no milk . . .
people	Shoo! Never come back, shoo! Shoo!
	People are dancing, waving their hands back and forth and lifting their feet up and down, feeling pulse

159

on their shoulders and turning their necks around
as if they were dancing in *kut* or in festival.

from heaven. . . crying and fretting,
the baby still grows up
when famine comes . . .

people   Shoo, shoo! Never come back, shoo! Shoo!

Getting spirited more and more,
heaven and earth
are dancing together
slowly.

--the end[3)]

The ones who crawled in the history of suffering could also dance because they dreamt of a new world symbolized in the legend of baby generalissimo and the dragon-horse. The expression, "Shoo, shoo! Never come back!" is paradoxical. Its literal meaning refers to a gesture to shoo birds away. Yet, in it is hidden people's messianic aspiration for the coming of a new world. Why did the writer change the tragic end of the original legend? I suspect the change reflects the Korean *minjung*'s expectation that their dynamic energy will be shaped by the new 'Gestalt of grace' brought by the Christian mission at the end of the last dynasty. According to the writer, "(The changed) symbol structure of the legend is the same as the structure of Jesus' life--the coming of the absolute, a short life in evil world, martyrdom and ascension as well as the Passover theme of Exodus in the Old Testament." The people's 'spirited' dancing is depicted as a new harmony between heaven and earth. Their cry of shooing sounds like their cry for the coming of a new heaven and earth. Shooing birds is paradoxically interrelated with welcoming birds. Birds symbolize divine presence in Shamanism and spiritual presence in Christianity.

The anamnesis of the motif of child killing in the legend indicts the Korean history of the crime of suppressing the *minjung*'s aspirations for the messianic kingdom. The story of Jesus' birth in the Gospel of Matthew also has the motif of child killing. The birth of Jesus means God has blood ties with humankind to give eternal life in the midst of bloodthirsty history. In the Magnificat, Mary praises God for the liberation of the poor, the downtrodden, and the oppressed.

My soul praises the Lord
and my spirit rejoices in God my Savior,
for he has been mindful of the humble state of his servant.
From now on all generations will call me blessed,
for the Mighty One has done great things for me--
holy is his name.
His mercy extends to those who fear him,
from generation to generation.
He has performed mighty deeds with his arms;
he has scattered those who are proud in their
inmost thoughts.
He has brought down rulers from their thrones
but he has lifted up the humble.
He has filled the hungry with good things
but has sent the rich away empty.
He has helped his servant Israel,
remembering to be merciful
to Abraham and his descendants forever,
even as he said to our fathers (Luke 1:46-55).

The story of the birth of Jesus provides us with a clue to healing the pathological *han* which has been the fundamental complex within the Korean psyche and has been caused by the fratricide and child killing of patriarchal rule for the last seven hundred years. The neo-neo-Confucian system of division did not allow any progressive politics within the South Korean political arena. Thus the radical students have become the major targets of fratricide and child killing by the military patriarchal rule. The conflict between military power and the power of the students has dominated Korean politics because of the limited political participation of middle-class citizens. When I came back to Korea in 1986 after I finished my theological study in the United States, the radical students' demonstration against the Chun regime, which took power after crushing the Kwangju *minjung* uprising, was approaching its peak. In the conclusion of my Ph.D. dissertation, "Paul Tillich's Categories for the Interpretation of History: An Application to the Encounter of Eastern and Western Cultures," I wrote:

The tragic denial of political power to the Korean masses has been the main obstacle against the democratic development of Korean politics. The complete repression of political movements of the dynamic masses consolidates the dictatorial regimes in the forms of both ideologies. Instead of democracy (or the rule of the dynamic masses) either military technocracy or communist dictatorship suffocates the political freedom of the Korean

161

masses. This tragic denial of political power to the masses can be overcome by the latent bearers of the forms of democracy among religious-cultural as well as humanistic-political groups and movements outside of the main streams of official religions and official politics. Without the latent bearers of the forms of democracy, the vital forces of the dynamic masses are either suppressed to become *han* or demonically distorted to become the prey of communist or military chauvinism.

When I began teaching at the Methodist Theological Seminary in Seoul in the fall of 1986, I had to go out of the classrooms to the streets with my students to protect them and to protest for democracy. I suffered terrible tear gas so many times. In June 1987, a great number of middle-class citizens joined the students' demonstration. Anti-Americanism had spread among the radical students since the U.S. troops, which were in charge of every military operation in South Korea, did not abort General Chun's heavily armed soldiers' massacre in Kwangju. Around 1988 when South Korea decided to hold the Olympic Games, the students demanded that the government co-sponsor the Olympics with North Korea. And there appeared a tragic phenomenon among the radical students--a series of public suicide attempts. For instance, a student named Cho Sung-man, after shouting his anti-American protest and calling his mother, jumped from a high building at his college and killed himself. Later I happened to watch his funeral on videotape. When I saw the student's mother crying while embracing her son's coffin, a long-suppressed image of the weeping woman under the divine tree reappeared on the screen of my heart. But this time was different from the first time. I could not help but feel a deep *han*. The two mothers whose sons were killed by the neo-neo-Confucian system of division were the pieta of the contemporary Korean *minjung*. When the National Council of Churches in Korea announced the 1988 Declaration for Peace and Reunification of Korea, I was moved by its confession of the sin of hating and even cursing the North Korean communists as well as by its prophetic challenge to both North and South governments. Since then I have participated in the ecumenical praxis for the peace and reunification of Korea. Though sympathizing with the radical students' holy anger and their mothers' unbearable *han*, I found the students' option for the Ju-che socialism of the North pathetic as well as naive. As long as they remained addicted to authoritarian totalism, hidden in their masochistic drives, I considered it a symptom of the deep wounds in the Korean psyche as a whole.

A severe tension and conflict between the two lines of progressive social movements in Korean society has appeared since the second half of the 1980s. And *minjung* theology was challenged by critiques from both inside and outside. For some young *minjung* theologians the ambiguous notion of the *minjung* was an obstacle to their preferential option for the poor. Thus they tried to use Marx-Leninism as the methodological tool for analyzing the neo-colonial, state-monopoly capitalism in South Korea. For them the *minjung* only included workers, peasants, and the urban poor. It was clearly a class-oriented, materialistic reduction of *minjung* theology. As *minjung* theology staggered, a few theologians began to establish a theology of *minjok* (nation). Sympathizing with the pro-North Ju-che line of the radical students, *minjok* theologians argued that the struggle against national contradictions has priority over the struggle against class contradictions in the divided Korea and in the rest of the Third World. While the conflicts between PD (People's Democracy, indicating the *minjung*-liners) and NL (National Liberation, indicating the *minjok*-liners) went on without any creative and productive result, the breakdown of the Eastern bloc became a major blow to most progressive theologians in Korea.

To me the conflict of NL vs. PD was superficial because it occurred on the surface of the ideological conflict that was imposed on and internalized within the divided country. I felt a strong urge to search for an authentic alternative to Western theology in the profound depth of my people's spirituality. I understood the context of de-Westernizing theology in terms of a spiritual division which implied a religious-cultural division as well as an ideological conflict. My first book in Korean, *Interliving Theology* (1991), grew out of the Korean context of interkilling from which the *han*-cry of human beings, heaven, and earth constantly burst out. The metaphors of interkilling and interliving came from my encounter with the Korean minjung's religious traditions which exposed me to the spiritual wisdom of Koreans as well as their *han*. I would call this turn of my thought an amazing discovery of the paradigm of life which has been predominant among ecumenical theologians in the 1990s. Influenced by Kim Ji-ha, I could delve into the spiritual depth of the nineteenth century's Korean *minjung* messianic movement, Donghak. According Suun, the founder of Donghak, the state of *han* is the state in which the *ki* (vital forces of life) is repressed and all beings fall into the law of interkilling. When the supreme *ki* (Spirit) of God becomes present in one's spirit and one is awakened to the internal witness of God within, the vital forces of a new life and a new being bring *kaebyuk* (the new beginning of the latter heaven and earth). My recent interest in Korean theology of the Spirit has grown out of my interpretation of the experiences and life of the Korean church in light of the paradigm of life and interliving.

3. Hand in Hand, Crossing the Barrier: Life Dancing in the Spirit

The eighth WCC assembly of this century in Harare, Zimbabwe, will celebrate the fiftieth anniversary of the founding of the World Council of Churches. It is a Jubilee assembly to repent of the five-hundred-year-long history of colonialistic Christianity and to seek a vision of reconciliation and hope for the third millennium. It remains to be seen whether Christianity can unchain itself from its colonialistic past, prophetically challenge the ever-increasing power of the world capitalist system, and care for the victims of the system. Ten years have elapsed since the National Council of Churches in Korea suggested launching a Jubilee year movement in the spirit of Jesus' proclamation of the Jubilee year in Luke 4. During the last ten years a great change has occurred in the world surrounding the Korean peninsula; i.e., the Cold War is over and the new world order of economic systems is increasing its power. The 'Hot War' between the rich countries and the poor countries has taken the place of the Cold War. The globalization dominated by transnational corporations has divided the world into the haves (20%) and the have-nots (80%). The recent Korean economic crises as well as that of a few Southeast Asian countries clearly demonstrated the nature of globalization as unlimited competition dominated by the economic powers.

Globalization is not always negative. It can be positive, too. The overcoming of the system of division in Korea is possible only through a positive globalization, namely, an authentic ecumenism. Negative globalization has as its model the tower of Babel which imposes on the world one language and one system. Positive globalization calls for a model of Pentecostal ecumenism, which allows people various languages and various systems while seeking local autonomy as well as solidarity. Jesus began his ministry by proclaiming the coming of the Spirit of the Lord for the poor. Because the Korean Assembly of God joined the NCCK in 1997, the NCCK's proclamation of the Jubilee year had to deal with the issue of Pentecostal spirituality and ecumenical justice. In the Lukan text, Jesus' proclamation of the Jubilee year in Luke 4 is closely related to Pentecost in Acts 2. In the Korean church, the ecumenical group which supports the NCCK's proclamation of the Jubilee year and the evangelical group which identifies itself with Pentecostalism have been opposed to each other. The theological task of the contemporary Korean Holy Spirit movement is to launch a Jubilee Pentecostalism or a Pentecostal ecumenism which combines Jesus' message of the Jubilee year with Pentecost.

When the day of Pentecost came, they were all together in one place. Suddenly a sound like the blowing of a violent wind came from heaven and filled the whole house where they were sitting. They saw what seemed to be tongues of fire that separated and came to rest on each of them. All of them were filled with the Holy Spirit and began to speak in other tongues as the Spirit enabled them. . . . All the believers were together and had everything in common. Selling their possessions and goods, they gave to anyone as he had need (Acts 2:1-4, 44-45).

Pentecost was the starting point of the globalization of Jesus' movement. There were two kinds of globalization. One aimed at Pax Romana, and the other at Pax Christi. Pax Romana was achieved through the domination, monopoly, and hate by the minority which was imperial Rome. Pax Christi was the way of the cross which invited people from the periphery to share with and love one another. After Pentecost, Jesus' disciples witnessed to the Gospel with courage. Without the resurrection of the crucified Lord, Pentecost was not possible. And the change of the disciples from cowards to brave witnesses was not possible without Pentecost. A Taiwanese hymn well describes the change brought by Pentecost.

Holy Spirit giv'n to us, at Pentecost to found our Church.
Hearts were changed and fear destroyed, they who witnessed the Risen Lord.
Spirit true! Help us now, may we know your strength divine,
Bravely face the powers of evil, Christ's great vict'ry preach to all.[4]

It is significant to notice that the theological motif of Luke-Acts is analogous to that of the Sinai pericope. The Crucifixion of Jesus is considered the sacrifice of the Passover Lamb. And the coming of the Holy Spirit is considered the celebration of the Feast of Harvest with the firstfruits of the crops. There is a very strong emphasis on the necessity of sacrificing the Passover Lamb for the coming of the Holy Spirit. Here the harvest signifies the eschatological sign that Peter mentioned by quoting the prophet Joel: "In the last days, God says, I will pour out my Spirit on all people. Your sons and daughters will prophesy, your young men will see visions, your old men will dream dreams" (Acts 2:17). The globalization of the Gospel described in Pentecost is not so much the starting place as it is the ideal goal of the Christian community. The Lukan account of an outbreak of glossolalia and miraculous speech in many languages is "an account of the Gospel's spread as actually accomplished by a miraculous, eschatological act of God."[5] The ideal of every Christian community depicted in Acts 2 contradicts the logic of domination, manipulation, and monopoly which is the rule of the world system of money and power. Miraculous speech refers to the ideal speech for Christian communicative praxis and the sharing of all possessions to bring about the vision of an alternative community free from monopoly and partiality.

Pentecost for the contemporary Korean church signifies the positive globalization of the Jubilee movement for peace and reunification of Korea over against the negative globalization of the world system. In Korea today there is a double plague--the plague of money in the South and the plague of food in the North. The North is so anxious to preserve the status quo that it spends an enormous amount on the military while people are starving to death. The extreme lack of food in the North is dramatically contrasted with the extreme waste of food in the South. The system of division as the subsystem of world capitalism holds sway over Korea. The beggarly capitalism in Korea has the Shamanistic and Confucian ethos. Korea, Taiwan, and China have followed the secret of Japan's economic growth and the government's role in it. President Park's regime of October Restoration imitated the Meiji Restoration in 1868 in the sense that it provided a great role for the nation-state in industrialization and economic growth. Following the pre-War Japanese model of a state-sponsored and state-led development, the authoritarian government of South Korea widened its role in the development process. However, unlike its Japanese or Taiwanese counterpart, Korean capitalism has its uniquely Shamanistic ethos.

The Shamanistic ethos of Korean capitalism has three traits. First, Koreans tend to work hard as if they were grasped by the Spirit. It is no wonder that such a Shamanistic ethos goes along with Pentecostalism which guarantees material blessing. The rapid post-War economic development of South Korea was greatly indebted to the Korean *minjung*'s dynamic power to overcome the soul-diminishing poverty that had dominated the long history of Korea. For them, material well-being is not a base materialism but a quasi-messianic hope of release from an age-old economic deprivation which prevented any control over their destiny and made them the victims of the *han*-reinforcing mechanism of domination. Shamanistic capitalism's 'spirited' diligence is analogous to the Protestant ethos of modern Western capitalism which is well described by John Wesley's first rule for the use of money; i.e., gain all you can as long as your work does not harm the soul and the body of oneself and his or her neighbors. Nevertheless, this Shamanistic ethos of Korean capitalism should not be imposed on other people who have different religious-cultural backgrounds. For instance, the spiritual diversity of foreign migrant workers in Korea should be respected by the Korean church in her mission

166

and evangelism for them. This is the spirit of Pentecostal ecumenism or of ecumenical Pentecostalism. The original day of Pentecost was the day of festivity after the harvest of first crops. The day of Pentecost in Acts also reflects its elements of festivity celebrating unity in diversity. In the Shamanistic tradition, work and dance are not two opposites. They are rather two sides of one coin. It is important to note that the two motifs of Shamanistic culture are *han* and *shin-myung*. *Shin-myung* is the burst of energy that allows the crippled to dance and that springs out through the dance. *Shin-myung* is the enhanced fulfilment of life energy that transforms all forces of interkilling into a newer and greater power of interliving.

> *Saeng-myung* (life) is *shin-myung* in other words. *Shin-myung* is precisely the subject and basis of work and dance. Without *shin-myung*, we could neither work nor dance. Without it, work is like forced slave labor. Without it, dance would be a dance of compulsion.[6]

The second trait of the Shamanistic ethos of Korean capitalism is that Koreans tend to hide their real names when they save what they gain in banks. The *minjung*'s distrust of any public agency was caused by the long history of corrupt government in Korea. The lack of transparency of government policy also caused a distortion of the communal nature of *shin*-myung so that the underground economy increased quickly. And the loss of *shin-myung* among the *minjung* results in a beggarly capitalism which seeks economic value at the cost of life value. The first iniquity of such capitalism is the fall of the Korean Ananias and Sapphira.

When Ananias and his wife kept back part of the money for themselves, Peter scolded them by saying that they "have lied to the Holy Spirit" (Acts 5:3). Then they fell down and died, and "Great fear seized the whole church" (Acts 5:11). Korean Christians are very much like Ananias and Sapphira. What shall they do? First and foremost they have to learn to distinguish the love of money from the use of money. One cannot and should not serve God and Mammom. "The love of money is the root of all evil" (1 Timothy 6:10). Wesley points out that the love of money has been, in all ages, the principal cause of the decay of true Christian faith:

> "As money increases, so does the love of it"--and always will, without a miracle of grace. Although there may also be other causes, this has been in all ages the principal cause of the decay of true religion in every Christian community. As long as the Christians in any place were poor they were devoted to God. While they had little of the world they did not love the world; but the more they had of it the more they loved it.

This constrained the Lover of their souls at various times to unchain their persecutors, who by reducing them to their former poverty reduced them to their former purity. But still remember: riches have in all ages been the bane of genuine Christianity.[7]

It is well known that Wesley had two other rules for the use of money besides "Gain all you can." "Save all you can" without wasting money for gratifying the desires of the flesh, the desires of the eye, and the pride of life. And "Give all you can" and do not bury it in the earth. It is interesting to note that Wesley considers hiding money in a chest or saving it in the Bank of England the same as burying it in the earth! Because "not to use is effectually to throw it away," genuine Christians ought to add the third rule to the two preceding. Wesley's rules for the use of money are useful for Korean Christians to prevent Shamanistic capitalism from falling into beggarly capitalism. Korean Christians have to lean how to act not as a proprietor but as a steward of the Lord.

The third trait of the Shamanistic ethos of Korean capitalism is that Koreans tend to overspend themselves in order to resolve their *han*. During the last year (1997) more than ten billion dollars worth of food waste was thrown away in the South while several million people were starving to death in the North. Though a few NGOs, including the Korean church, have been sending food to the North, the South Korean government has not allowed any food campaign for the North through the mass media. It has been reported that church leaders in the North have repeatedly said to their visitors from the South, "If you don't help us now, how will you dare face the people of the North when Korea is reunited?" It is no wonder that many conscientious Christians consider the present economic crisis to be divine wrath. Korean Christians should fear the Lord in this situation instead of worrying about the rise in prices and the loss of jobs. They have to fear the Lord not because they might become poor again but because they might not recover the purity of their faith. The second iniquity of Korean capitalism is its partiality in the distribution of wealth. Such iniquity also existed in the early church. Even after the incident of Ananias and Sapphira, there was a conflict between the Grecian Jews and the Aramaic-speaking Jews because the widows of the Grecian Jews were overlooked in the daily distribution of food. It was a manifest breach of brotherly love in the Aramaic-speaking Jews, a sin against justice and mercy. The plague of partiality produced another plague of resentment among the Grecian Jews. God's last remedy for this first crisis of division in the earthly church was persecution. Wesley describes its happy effect in Acts 9:

Both the partiality of the Hebrews ceased, and the murmuring of the Grecians. And "then churches rest, and were edified," built up in the love of God and one another. "And walking in the fear of the Lord, and in the comforts of the Holy Ghost, were multiplied" (Acts 9:31).[8]

Thus far the economic growth of South Korea has been a partial one based on the system of division working for interkilling. If both North and South reduce their enormous military spending for interkilling, and the capital and technology of the South is combined with the natural resources and labor force of the North, a new paradigm of Jubilee economy can create a path to the peaceful reunification of Korea working for interliving. The double plague of the food crisis in the North and state bankruptcy in the South could be indeed a blessed opportunity for the life of wandering in the wilderness until we enter the promised land of reunited Korea. The mutual reduction of armaments in both the South and the North is the only way not to perish together but to live together, not to interkill but to interlive. Pax American in the Korean peninsula has to be replaced by Pax Christi. The military expenditures of both South and North are threatening their economic survival. The military expenditures of South Korea have increased from 8.5 billion dollars in 1990 to 18 billion dollars in 1997.[9] Despite the high rate of economic growth, the portion of expenditures for social welfare is only 2.6% of the GNP, because South Korea had to buy very expensive armaments from the United States. Economic specialists assume that more than 1.5 million persons will lose their jobs in 1998 which is the first year of the era of the IMF relief fund. But a budget for unemployment compensation is not enough. The reduction of military expenditures will have a double effect. It will not only achieve peace in the Korean peninsula but also stimulate economic recovery.

Just as the Korean church led the spiritual reform of the nation in 1907 when Korea faced the loss of its national sovereignty, the contemporary Korean church has to lead another spiritual reform of the nation. First of all, we have to turn to God and walk in the fear of the Lord. This is the time to declare a fast and to put on sackcloth and to sit down in the dust. Jonah's message of the wrath of God has been too-long swallowed by the illusion of an advanced country. But the great fish cannot help but vomit him up so that a message against the system of division can be heard. The wrath of God is indeed the mercy of God. "Blessed are those who mourn, for they will be comforted" (Matthew 5:4). If we turn to God and walk in the fear of the Lord, "God may yet relent and with compassion turn from his fierce anger so that we will not perish" (Jonah 3:9). Indeed, only when

169

we walk in the fear of the Lord, then may we also walk in the comforts of the Holy Spirit.

The recent document of the WCC, "Towards a Common Understanding and Vision of the WCC," describes well the changing context: "While nearly two-thirds of the churches which founded the WCC came from Europe and North America, nearly two-thirds of the member churches today come from Africa, Asia, the Caribbean, Latin America, the Middle East and the Pacific, making the Council more truly a world body."[10] The globalizing influence of the world system dominated by the trilateral North (the United States, Japan, and the European Union) is becoming greater and greater in the Third World. The crisis of foreign debt in the Third World has reached its limit. The eighth assembly of the WCC has been prepared "in a spirit of Jubilee--that is, of repentance and renewal of life." An ecumenical Jubilee could be realized by forgiving the enormous debts of the poor countries. The revitalization of the Jubilee theme is indeed the Korean church's contribution to the ecumenical movement. Furthermore, the Korean church is located in the boundary between the North and the South. It is up to the Korean church whether she becomes the peacemaker between the two in this world of limitless competition or the oppressed turning into the oppressor. Then the Korean church's struggle to overcome the neo-neo-Confucian system of division has global and ecumenical significance. It could become the struggle of the bride of the Lamb over against the Woman on the Beast. The Woman on the world system seems to rule the system of division, yet eventually the followers of the Lamb will witness the fall of Babylon the Great and the coming down of the new heaven and the new earth:

> Fallen! Fallen is Babylon the Great!
> She has become a home for demons
> and a haunt for every evil spirit,
> a haunt for every unclean and detestable bird.
> For all the nations have drunk
> the maddening wine of her adulteries.
> The kings of the earth committed adultery with her,
> and the merchants of the earth grew rich from her
> excessive luxuries (Revelation 18:2-3).

> Hallelujah!
> For our Lord God Almighty reigns.
> Let us rejoice and be glad
> and give him glory!
> For the wedding of the Lamb has come,

170

and his bride has made herself ready.
Fine linen, bright and clean,
was given her to wear (Revelation 19:7-8).

In the Babylonian captivity of the present world there is no barrier of region, culture, race, or nation-state. Every phase of our life is commercialized. The world system produces marginalized beings all over the world. They are the crawling ones who are invited by the angel to dance in the Spirit till the wedding supper of the Lamb. The crawling person is the marginalized person in the midst of our globally-oriented society where many different cultural and ethnic communities are supposed to coexist for interliving. A marginal person lives in two cultures and is a member of neither. Yet it is not the dominant group's either/or way of life but the marginal person's neither/nor experience (interkilling experience) that can be transformed into the creative both/and (interliving) life style. You can say that the kind of life which always flies over and steps on others belongs to the either/or life of interkilling which is related to a two-beat theology drumming for endless marching. In this theology, God and the human, the human and the human, the human and the world, and the world and God are involved in the permanent damnation of interkilling. Life built on such a theology cannot help but end up with eternal boredom or two-beat rhythm. But what about the crawling life, or the kind of life which is lived through solidarity with the crawling ones? The grace of the God crawling in Jesus Christ the Lamb turns the crawling one's wailing into the dancing of the bride of the Lamb through the Spirit's mysterious fellowship, namely, through creating a marginal beat or fuzzy beat between the two extreme beats that mutually contradict. This is what I mean by a three-beat theology of the Spirit that creates a gap against the gap caused by Satan. Life related to such a theology for cosmic and historical divine-human participation moves with wonder and excitement despite its *han* cry and guilt. Every step you take will turn out to be a step forward for the interliving between God and the human. Every line your hands draw will turn out to be a move to reconcile heaven and earth. Let's crawl with God and dance in the Spirit!

1) Cf. Yun Sung-bum, *Korean Theology* (Seoul: Sunmyungmunwhasa, 1972).

2) Cf. Paik Nak-chung, "For Understanding the System of Division," *Writing and Criticism* 78, 1992 Winter.

3) Choi Yin-hoo, *Good Old Days, Shoo! Shoo!* (Seoul: Munhakkwajisungsa, 1997), 120-121.

4) Cf. *Sound the Bamboo: CCA Hymnal 1990*, No. 152.

5) Hans Conzelmann, *A Commentary on the Acts of the Apostles* (Philadelphia: Fortress Press, 1987), 15.

6) Kim Ji-ha, *Rice* (Seoul: Bundo Publishing House, 1993), 96.

7) Albert Outler, ed., *The Works of John Wesley* Vol. 2 (Nashville: Abingdon Press, 1985), 468.

8) Ibid., 457.

9)Cf. *The Han-Kyoreh Daily News Paper*, Jan. 10, 1998, 1.

10) *The Ecumenical Review* Vol. 49, No. 1, Jan. 1997, 15.